D0992331

JEWS AND THE QUR'AN

Jews and the Qur'an

MEIR M. BAR-ASHER

TRANSLATED BY
ETHAN RUNDELL

WITH A FOREWORD BY
MUSTAFA AKYOL, AUTHOR OF
THE ISLAMIC JESUS

PREFACE BY
MOHAMMAD ALI AMIR-MOEZZI

PRINCETON UNIVERSITY PRESS
PRINCETON & OXFORD

English translation copyright © 2021 by Princeton University Press

Princeton University Press is committed to the protection of copyright and the intellectual property our authors entrust to us. Copyright promotes the progress and integrity of knowledge. Thank you for supporting free speech and the global exchange of ideas by purchasing an authorized edition of this book. If you wish to reproduce or distribute any part of it in any form, please obtain permission.

Requests for permission to reproduce material from this work should be sent to permissions@press.princeton.edu

Published by Princeton University Press
41 William Street, Princeton, New Jersey 08540
6 Oxford Street, Woodstock, Oxfordshire OX20 1TR

press.princeton.edu

All Rights Reserved
Originally published as *Les Juifs dans le Coran*
© Editions Albin Michel—Paris 2019
ISBN 978-0-691-21135-0
ISBN (e-book) 978-0-691-23258-4

Library of Congress Control Number: 2021945070

British Library Cataloging-in-Publication Data is available

Editorial: Fred Appel and James Collier
Production Editorial: Karen Carter
Jacket/Cover Design: Layla Mac Rory
Production: Erin Suydam
Publicity: Kate Hensley and Kathryn Stevens

Jacket/Cover Credit: Tile panel with verses from the Qur'an. Once a decorative part of an architectural monument in Iznik, Turkey. 16th century / The Walters Art Museum, Baltimore, MD

This book has been composed in Arno

Printed on acid-free paper. ∞

Printed in the United States of America

10 9 8 7 6 5 4 3 2 1

In memory of my dear sisters, Hadassa and Sima.

CONTENTS

Mustafa Akyol

IN THE SECOND HALF of the twentieth century, it became fashionable in the West to speak of "the Judeo-Christian tradition." The term referred to a fact that most Christians had not acknowledged for almost two millennia: that Christianity was born out of Judaism—by inheriting it, universalizing it, but also struggling with it, at times through hostility and oppression.

There is a similarly valid "Judeo-Islamic tradition" which has not yet received the attention it deserves. For, Islam, too, claims the heritage of the Jewish patriarchs and prophets—Abraham and his sons, as well as Joseph or Moses—and even adds a self-acclaimed mission to universalize their faith to all humanity. Moreover, Islam proves even closer to Judaism than to Christianity in its theology and practice. Its theology is a strict monotheism that has no place for a divine messiah, graven images, or "being saved by grace"—unlike Christianity, but just like Judaism. And its practice is defined by Islam's legal tradition, Sharia, which is unmistakably modeled on the Jewish legal tradition, Halakha.

In addition, until the modern era the fate of Jews in the lands of Islam was often more tolerable than that of Christians. This explains why some Jews in territories with a Christian majority, such as Catholic Spain, fled to majority-Muslim lands, such as the Ottoman Empire. The latter's capital, Istanbul, my hometown, was for centuries "unquestionably the best place in the world for Jews to live," as historian Alan Mikhail puts it.

Yet one also can see in the birth pangs of the new religion of Islam a tension between it and Judaism. For it is the inevitable calling of every new religion to explain what went wrong before it appeared; namely, the errors it has come to correct. And while early Islam's main nemesis was polytheism, it had to mark its divergences from Christianity and Judaism as well, although in different and interesting ways.

In this meticulously written and highly readable book, Meir M. Bar-Asher masterfully portrays this complex relation between Judaism and Islam, by focusing on how the latter—at its core, the Qur'an—sees the former. (Judaism's view of Islam would also be an interesting story, but that would be another book.) He is right to argue, I believe, that this is a relation full of "ambiguity." On the one hand, "there are the positive declarations" in the Qur'an about Israelites as God's chosen people who upheld his earlier revelation, the Torah, to which Qur'an shows utmost respect. On the other hand, the same Israelites— and their Jewish descendants—are depicted as a people that broke their Covenant with God, corrupted the Torah (or at least its interpretations), and also acted treacherously toward the early Muslim community.

As Bar-Asher shows, the same ambiguity characterizes the Qur'anic attitude toward Jewish religious practices. On the one hand, Islam adopts various aspects of the Jewish Law, such as the prohibition of pork, blood, and carrion. On the other hand, it shows "a deliberate desire to draw away from Judaism," evidenced in its rejection of the more complicated details of Jewish dietary laws, and in its fateful change of the direction of Islamic prayer from Jerusalem to Mecca.

I believe that this objective assessment of Jews in the Qur'an will be a contribution not only to scholarship on Jewish-Muslim relations, but also to a broader understanding of that relationship. In recent times, popular books published in Western countries have been saturated with efforts to depict Islam—unfairly and inaccurately—as either a hopelessly anti-Semitic creed, or as a utopia of interfaith co-existence. The truth is certainly more complex, as Bar-Asher shows in his analysis.

To me, and to other Muslims who believe there should be no enmity toward anyone without a good reason, a nuanced approach of this kind is helpful in reconciling seemingly antagonistic Qur'anic verses concerning relations between Muslims and other peoples. One of them, verse 5:51, discussed more than once in Bar-Asher's book, reads as follows: "O you who believe, do not take the Jews and the Christians as friends. They are friends of each other." But this forbidding advice is balanced by verse 60:8: "[God] does not forbid you to deal kindly and justly with anyone who has not fought you for your faith or driven you out of your homes." Cases such as these, in which the Qur'an appears to be interpreting itself, helps us put seemingly intolerant commandments into a broader framework of fairness—unless the magnanimous verses are considered to be "abrogated" by the antagonistic ones, as quite a few traditional exegetes have unfortunately suggested.

I would also underline another important point captured in this book: the "ambiguity" of the Qur'an concerning Jews and Judaism has made it easy for Muslims to be selective in their approach to the issue—and throughout Islamic history political context has played a decisive role in their choices. In the modern era, the toxic politics surrounding the Arab-Israeli conflict led to a re-reading of the Qur'an, and the life of the Prophet, that generated a decidedly dark portrait of Jews. That is why, as Bar-Asher puts it, "traditional [Islamic] exegesis tended to focus more on specifying the circumstances in which a given verse applied whereas the modern tendency is to absolutize its meaning and transform it into an ideological weapon." He also shows how this "ideological weapon" works in the narratives of militant groups such as Hamas.

Yet, I am happy to add, a different trend is gaining momentum among Muslim minority communities in Western countries, in which Jews are seen not as rebellious dhimmis or perfidious conspirators but instead as a fellow minority facing similar challenges. I am thinking in particular of white supremacists in the United States, whose venom threatens both synagogues and mosques, and of intrusive laws in Europe that encroach on such religious practices of both Jews and Muslims as circumcision, or the kosher and halal slaughter of animals. Consequently, perhaps for the first time in their history, Jews and Muslims are seeking religious tolerance and freedom together, and beginning to discover their commonalities as fellow Semites in a gentile world.

I hope that this new chapter in history may bring about better understanding between Jews and Muslims, a goal that would be greatly advanced by the kind of scholarly rigor and objectivity that I have found in Meir Bar-Asher's *Jews and the Qur'an*. I have read the book with great interest, and I see in it an informative basis for frank dialogue between the children of Abraham—no matter how deep-seated their intra-family issues.

Mustafa Akyol
Senior Fellow on Islam and Modernity
Cato Institute

PREFACE

AT A TIME when the question of Islam's attitude toward the Jews is often foregrounded in the media, books such as this one are indispensable. In the clash between those who promote the notion that the Qur'an is "antisemitic" (sometimes without having read it) and those who, with the help of a few carefully chosen Qur'anic verses, seek to demonstrate to their flock the "perfidious" nature of the Jews, a more objective approach is lost. While Islam cannot be reduced to the Qur'an, the latter nevertheless remains its foundation stone. Yet one must be capable of reading it seriously, taking it into account as a complex whole, and paying attention to its contexts. One must also be skilled in untangling the ways in which various forms of classical and modern Islam have drawn upon the Qur'an in developing their discourse on Jews and Judaism, always keeping historical circumstances in mind.

For nearly two centuries, Orientalists and Arabists have been intrigued by the outsized presence in the Qur'an of elements belonging to, or originating in, Judaism. From Abraham Geiger's study, *Was hat Mohammed aus dem Judenthume aufgenommen?* which appeared in the first half of the nineteenth century, and Gabriel Said Reynolds' book, *The Qur'an and the Bible: Text and Commentary* (2018), to the work of such accomplished scholars as Ignaz Goldziher, David Sidersky, Shlomo Dov Goitein, Patricia Crone, Michael Cook, Uri Rubin, Michael Lecker,

Sidney Griffith, and many others, critical research has drawn upon historically and philologically rigorous methods to open new avenues for study, provoke fascinating debate, and demonstrate the huge complexity of the issues under consideration. What form(s) of Judaism are we talking about? Which currents and which religious sources could have influenced the Qur'an? Focusing on the religion of those Jews who remained faithful to such Jewish beliefs and practices as circumcision, the celebration of Shabbat, and the prohibition on consuming pork, but who simultaneously believed in Jesus as Savior at the end of time, what is known as the "Judeo-Christian" avenue of research appears fertile. Here, too, there have been many studies, from those of Hans-Joachim Schoeps and M. P. Roncaglia to Carlos Sogovia, Shlomo Pines, and Giuseppe Rizzardi. In the recently edited volume in tribute to Patricia Crone, Guy G. Stroumsa supplies a scholarly historiography of this research. Meanwhile, in his imposing survey *Les disciples juifs de Jésus du 1er siècle à Mahomet* (Paris, 2017), Dominique Bernard shows that Ebionites/Nazarenes were actively present in the first centuries of the *hijra* and within the Muslim community.

The whys and wherefores, the implications and avenues for investigating these issues are many. The first questions they raise concern nothing less than the religion of Muhammad himself. What was the religious environment of his birth and education? Upon which tradition(s) did he draw to quench his spiritual thirst? Contrary to what Muslim apologetics would later claim, pre-Islamic Arabia was not an "era of ignorance" and idolatry, nor did Islam initiate Arab monotheism. Idolatry probably had ceased to exist many centuries earlier, except perhaps among a few nomadic Bedouins.

Numerous studies by scholars such as Frédéric Imbert, Christian Robin, and Jan Retsö have extensively documented this fact, especially outside the Hejaz. The strongest textual confirmation, however, comes from the Qur'an itself. It includes: the massive presence of Old and New Testament figures; the allusive nature of its biblical stories (indicating a close familiarity on the part of its audience with these stories, since such allusions would otherwise have been unintelligible); the onomastic evidence of biblical names with origins in the East Christianities of Syro-Palestine; the Hebraic, Aramaic, and Syriac roots of such focal terms as *qur'an*, *sura* (a chapter of the Qur'an), *aya* (a Qur'anic verse), *zakat* (alms-giving), *ṣalat* (canonical prayer), *ḥajj* (the great pilgrimage to Mecca), and *'umra* (the lesser pilgrimage to Mecca).

In the present book, Meir M. Bar-Asher brilliantly rises to the challenge of summarizing earlier studies, while at the same time advancing relevant new questions. He is doubtless among the contemporary scholars best suited to an undertaking of this nature. A preeminent expert on Islam and Judaism with a perfect mastery of the relevant languages, a shrewd analyst of the thought and spirituality of both religions, and an historian and philologist, he has also a great gift for transmitting his knowledge of very difficult subjects in a clear and accessible manner. As a specialist of Shi'ism, I am particularly pleased to note that he devotes an important chapter to this branch of Islam, the "poor cousin" of Islamic studies (notwithstanding some noteworthy advances in recent years). Students and established scholars alike will find this book of immense value, as will any educated reader with an interest in the subject.

Mohammad Ali AMIR-MOEZZI
École Pratique des Hautes Études (Sorbonne)

ACKNOWLEDGMENTS

THE PRESENT BOOK originated in a conference I gave in Paris in 2015 on the theme "Islam and the Torah of Israel as Seen by the Qur'an and Ḥadith" at the invitation of my friend Professor Tony Lévy, an emeritus scholar at the CNRS and specialist on the history of mathematics. Also in attendance at the conference was Professor Mireille Hadas-Lebel, director of the "Présences du judaïsme poche" collection, who invited me to develop my thoughts at book length. I am grateful to them for this; it was they who convinced me to write the present book. More generally, the content of this book is drawn from two seminars I led, the first at the Paideia European Institute for Jewish Studies in Stockholm from 2007 to 2017, the second in Pilsen in the Czech Republic in 2012. Both were devoted to points of contact and friction between Islam and Judaism. The fruitful exchanges that took place with my colleagues and students, both over the course of these two seminars and on the occasion of other lectures I delivered on these themes over the years, were the source of many insights into this complex problem, and it is this deeper understanding that I hope to share with the readers of this book. I am indebted also to Professor Shmuel Trigano, with whom I held a colloquium in Paris in 2006 on the theme "Judaism and the Origins of Islam." I would also like to thank Dr. Julien Darmon for his great help in critically reading and improving the French version of this book.

JEWS AND THE QUR'AN

Introduction

THE PRESENT WORK seeks to consider the nature of the affinities between Islam and Judaism. To do so, it is indispensable to return to the sources—that is, to the issues at play in the Qur'an itself. As it is neither possible nor fair to consider the Qur'an in isolation from the literature to which it gave rise, however, I will also as far as possible consider the Islamic religious literature that draws its inspiration from the Qur'an: the oral tradition attributed to the Prophet of Islam, known as the Ḥadith; the commentaries on the Qur'an; the Islamic polemical literature against Judaism, and so on. The same dynamic characterizes Judaism, for the written and oral Torah are also inextricably mixed. Very often, it is impossible to understand Qur'anic text and context without appealing to the post-Qur'anic tradition. At the very least, this oral tradition allows us to grasp how, at various periods, Muslims understood the Qur'an. This is why all of this book's chapters call upon post-Qur'anic sources to varying degrees.

I have attempted to account for the Qur'anic relationship to the Jews across all of its shades and gradations, from the brightest to the most somber. Jews, their religion and their Holy Scriptures are quite frequently mentioned in the Qur'an. It recounts many well-known biblical episodes in close detail, some of them more than once. These include: the history of the Patriarchs; the servitude of the children of Israel in the land of Pharaoh; their departure from Egypt; their arrival and settling of the Holy Land; and the giving of the Torah. One also finds references to various miracles that occurred to the children of Israel during their time in the desert: the pillar of cloud that accompanied them; the manna from heaven; the quail that fell from the sky; and the water that sprang forth from a rock to slake the people's thirst.

The biblical figures whose stories are mentioned several times include those of Abraham and his family; Lot and his kin; Moses and the children of Israel's suffering in Egypt; and, in passing, the story of the scouts sent by Moses before entering the Promised Land; David and Solomon, Jonah (*Yunus*), also called *Dhu l-nun* (the man of the fish), Job (*Ayyub*), and many others.

It is not only the voices of the Bible's heroes that we hear in the Qur'an. Faith and law—public, private, and religious—all occupy a very prominent place in the text and all show extensive evidence of cross-pollination with Biblical and other Jewish sources. These we will discuss later.

First let us consider the extent and depth of the ties joining the Qur'an to the Bible and postbiblical Judaism, a question that has of course been much debated by scholars. In this book, I shall present the historical and cultural context in which Islam emerged by describing in detail Judaism as it was practiced by the Jews of Arabia at the time Muhammad began his prophetic career. As recounted by Muslim tradition, this period spanned twelve years, from 610 to 622, and follows Muhammad from Mecca, his birthplace, to Yathrib, later known as al-Madina (Medina). Muhammad is said to have come into contact with

Jews primarily in Medina and its surroundings, where he was active during the last ten years of his life, from 622 to 632. It was there that he learned their religion and history.

The book will first present the historical background of the encounter between Jews and Arabs in the centuries preceding the advent of Islam, mainly as related by Arab sources, and will later explore early relations between Jews and Muslims. We will then look at the image of Jews and Judaism presented by the Qur'an.

We shall begin by examining the terminology and various names by which the Qur'an refers to Jews. I shall identify the characteristics of each of these names and what they tell us about how the Jews and their religion were regarded. Three terms will receive particular attention: *banu isra'il* (the children of Israel, *al-yahud* (Jews) and *ahl al-kitab* (the People of the Book).

I will then note the various, contradictory ways in which the Qur'an depicts Jews and their religion. On the one hand, there are the positive declarations: the Israelites are presented as the chosen people upon whom God lavished his kindness, freeing them from slavery in Egypt, bestowing upon them the Torah, creating prophets in their midst, and leading them to the Promised Land. On the other hand, they are presented as a people that broke its Covenant with God, reverted to idolatry, falsified the God-given Torah, and killed the prophets sent to restore them to the straight and narrow path. In short, a people who, by virtue of having broken their Covenant with God, were unworthy of alliance: "O you who believe, do not take the Jews and Christians as friends. They are friends of each other" (Q. 5:51).[1]

The last two chapters, in particular, call for an additional word of explanation. Devoted to the "Qur'anic foundations of the legal status of Jews under Islamic domination," Chapter 5 might at first glance seem a doubtful fit in this book to the degree that it concerns politico-theological developments that took place after the Qur'anic source had achieved its final form. Its inclusion is nevertheless justified by the fact that this process, though not "Qur'anic" in itself, drew upon Qur'anic verses in elucidating the legal status of Jews and other religious minorities. The same goes for Chapter 6, devoted to "the place of Judaism and Jews in Twelver Shi'ism": while it is true that these are late developments in Islam, they appeal to notions that are in fact discussed in the Qur'an itself. This closing chapter also allows us to move beyond a strictly Sunni majoritarian vantage point to encompass the Shi'i world that, minoritarian though it may be, is none the less powerful. It is estimated that the various Shi'i branches count 150 million followers, or a tenth of the world's Muslim population; and within Shi'ism, the Twelver branch occupies by far the majority position today.

This book seeks to reveal the extent to which the two religions are inextricably entwined—at once close and distant, friendly and hostile. This ambivalence lies at the heart of Islam's relationship to Judaism and the Jews, and it assumes several aspects that are worth exploring. It may be detected in the Qur'an's complex attitude toward the Bible. On the one hand, the Qur'an sees the Bible as a text revealed by God to the human race and thus as a book capable of authenticating the revelation offered Muhammad in the Qur'an, as both have the same divine source. On the other hand, the Qur'an sees the Bible as a book given the Jews that lost its value after they knowingly altered it, among other reasons so as to remove all references to the future advent of Muhammad and the new religion he would bring into the world. It goes without saying that the Bible's falsification renders it inferior to the Qur'an, which is considered to be the authentic word of God. In other words, the Jews are as much

People of the Book (*ahl al-kitab*) as they are "an ass carrying books" (Q 62:5)—that is, a people bearing an immense heritage on their shoulders but of which they are ignorant and which, in reality, they do not deserve. The Qur'an's ambiguity vis-à-vis the biblical (and post-biblical) heritage is also evident in Qur'anic law. Everything that concerns prayer, fasting, dietary rules, purity, and impurity bears a clear relation to the Bible and post-biblical Jewish sources. Yet one also observes many laws that exhibit a deliberate desire to draw away from Judaism. Among the most striking examples, one may note the decision to shift the direction of prayer (*qibla*) from Jerusalem to Mecca, changes to the fasting (*ṣawm*) and dietary laws, and revisions to the calendar, a subject we will revisit.

The links between the Qur'an and the Bible have been noted from the earliest days of Islamic studies and the pioneering work of Abraham Geiger, best known as a founding father of the Jewish reformist movement in Germany. In 1833, he published his study, *Was hat Mohammed aus dem Judenthume aufgenommen?* (translated as, *Islam and Judaism*), in Bonn. A large number of scholars have followed his lead. I will only cite a few of them here, all of whom devoted major studies to the ties between Judaism and Islam. In his book, *Koranische Untersuchungen* (Qur'anic Studies), which appeared in Berlin and Leipzig in 1926, Josef Horovitz identified the various passages where the Qur'an and the biblical and post-biblical sources intersect. In *Die biblischen Erzählungen im Qoran* (Biblical Stories in the Qur'an), published in Hildesheim in 1961, Heinrich Speyer noted the many parallels between accounts in the Qur'an and those in the Bible and Talmudic literature. In the same vein, one may cite David Sidersky, *Les Origines des légendes musulmanes dans le Coran et les vies des prophètes* ("The

Origins of Muslim Legends in the Qur'an and the Lives of the Prophets").[2]

Closer to our times, one may mention the many articles by Sidney Griffith and, more particularly, his book, *The Bible in Arabic: The Scriptures of the "People of the Book" in the Language of Islam*, as well as the work of Uri Rubin, especially his *Between Bible and Qur'an*.[3] A major contribution was Jacqueline Chabbi's *Le Coran décrypté, Figures bibliques en Arabie* (Paris, 2008). Daniel Sibony authored a general study, *Coran et Bible en questions et réponses* (Paris, 2017), and most recently we have Gabriel S. Reynolds' book, *The Qur'an and the Bible: Text and Commentary* (New Haven, 2018). These are just a few of the titles to have appeared in this proliferating field over the past two centuries.

———

The Qur'anic citations used in this volume are from Alan Jones' translation of *The Qur'an* (Exeter, 2007), with slight modifications.

In order to facilitate the reading experience of non-specialists, I have adopted a simplified transcription that will be easily recognizable to Arabic scholars. For the benefit of the former, a few remarks regarding pronunciation: ' indicates the *hamza*, which corresponds to a glottal stop (e.g., the vowel between *uh-oh!*) and ' indicates, a guttural sound characteristic of Arabic and other Semitic languages; *gh* corresponds to the uvular pronunciation of *r* as in Parisian French; *ḥ* is pronounced as a pharyngeal (at the back of the throat); *kh* corresponds to the German *ch* (as in the word *Buch*); *q* is pronounced as an emphatic *k* (at the back of the throat); *s* is always unvoiced, as in *essay*, never as in *easy*; *ṣ* is realized as an emphatic *s* (at the back of the throat); and *th* corresponds to the English *th* as in *thing* and *dh* to the English *th* as in *this*.

For reasons of simplicity, dates exclusively follow the Gregorian calendar, without the addition of their equivalent in what is known as the *hijri* calendar.

I

The Historical Context

THE FIRST CONTACTS between Jews and Arabs took place in the southern reaches of the Arabian Peninsula nearly a thousand years before the advent of Islam. Before their advent upon the scene of universal history, the Arabs already had ties with the Jews, though little is known about them. As Gordon D. Newby has so aptly put it, what has been written on the subject of Jews in pre-Islamic Arabia contains "much . . . that is fantasy, much that is polemic and some that I shall call history."[1] In fact, most of our information comes from Muslim sources written in the eighth century or later—that is, well after the beginnings of Islam.

How Jews came to settle in Arabia is not clearly established by the historical sources. For the most part, our only information comes from legends tracing the Jewish presence to the sixth century BCE: according to a Yemeni Jewish legend, the first Jewish inhabitants arrived forty-two years before the destruction of the First Temple (586 BCE). When Ezra called on the people after the fall of Babylon to return to the land of Israel and help reconstruct the Temple, they refused because they had foreseen that the Second Temple would also be destroyed. According to the legend, Ezra responded by cursing them, dooming them to physical and spiritual poverty.[2]

Yemeni Jews traditionally connect the era of their settlement in the region with the biblical episode of Solomon and the Queen of Sheba (Saba), which is echoed by the Qur'an in sura 27 ("The Ants"). The country of Saba is generally thought to have been located on both sides of the mouth of the Red Sea—that is, between present-day Yemen and Ethiopia. According to Muslim legend, the Queen of Sheba, known as Bilqis, converted to Judaism, along with many of her court's dignitaries, before marrying Solomon. After a son was born to the royal couple, Solomon dispatched Jewish masters from the Holy Land to the kingdom of Saba in order to provide the prince with a good Jewish education. These educators were thus the first Jewish inhabitants of Yemen. Whether or not this legend and the many others that date the Jewish settlement to the biblical era are true, it cannot be denied that commercial ties existed between the southern Arabian Peninsula and the Holy Land several centuries before our era, as this is confirmed by a Sabaean inscription discovered in Yemen in 2008. According to another legend, the Jews arrived in the Arabian Peninsula, and particularly the region of the Hejaz, under the authority of Nabonidus, the last Babylonian king (556–539 BCE). Entering the region of the Hejaz, Nabonidus subjugated its inhabitants and settled in Tema' (*Tayma'*). He recounted the conquest in his own words: "I hide myself afar (*useriqanni*) from my city of Babylon (on) the road to Tayma', Dadanu, Padakku, Hibra, Iadiiu and as far as Latribu; ten years I went about amongst them (and) to my city of Babylon, I went not in."[3]

Most of the towns mentioned in Nabonidus' account are important places which Muslim sources inform us had Jews in the pre-Islamic period, prior to their expulsion by Muhammad: Tema' refers to Tayma', Dadanu to Dedan (present-day al-'Ula), Padakku to Fadak, Hibra to Khaybar, and Latribu to Yathrib (the future Medina). Scholars suppose that his army contained many Jews, whom one might accordingly deem the first Jewish inhabitants of northern and western Arabia. Though it seems quite a stretch to see this partial testimony as clear evidence for the earliest Jewish settlement in Arabia, we do know that there was a substantial Jewish presence a few centuries later in the region of the Hejaz, the cradle of Islam, probably due to the arrival of Jews following the destruction of the Second Temple in 70 CE.

A Jewish Kingdom in Arabia

One of the most important episodes in the fragmentary history of the Jewish presence in Arabia is that of the kingdom of Himyar. Scholars agree that the origins of this kingdom, located in the southwestern corner of the peninsula, date from 110 BCE. In 275, Himyar annexed Saba, took control of Hadramawt, and for the first time unified southern Arabia under a single kingdom following more than a thousand years of cultural and political division. A hundred years later (370 CE), Himyar adopted monotheism in its Jewish version. Between the fourth and the sixth centuries, the Himyarites extended their influence over central and eastern Arabia, reaching Yamama and the neighborhood of Mecca. Himyar's emissaries established ties with the Arab tribes in these lands and launched military expeditions against other tribes. In the fifth century, the Himyarites appointed as their king Hujr Akil al-murar of southern Arabia's Kinda tribe, and his authority subsequently spread to other tribes of the region. His lineage retained the throne until the end of the sixth century.

The kingdom of Himyar was innovative not just in terms of its expansion, but also by virtue of the way in which it conceived of the state: whereas all earlier southern Arabian states had based their rule on the practice of a divine cult, through which they also affirmed their identity, loyalty to the king supplied the basis for Ḥimyar unification. It was the condition that that enabled fifth-century Yemenis to possess a centralized government, a shared language—Sabaean, which belonged to the same family as the Ethiopian languages but was far removed from Arabic—and a shared system of writing, South Arabic.

In the fourth century CE, the leaders of Ethiopia, then known as Aksum, converted to Christianity and drew closer to Byzantium. In the same period, and perhaps in response to the Ethiopian decision to adopt Christianity, the leaders of Ḥimyar converted to Judaism. This region at the mouth of the Red Sea was the scene of a proxy war between the Byzantine and Persian empires, with Christian Ethiopia allied with Byzantium and Ḥimyar supported by the Persians.[4] In the sixth century, the Ethiopians maneuvered to overthrow the Jewish king and replace him with a Christian, an effort in which they briefly succeeded (from 518 to 522). The spread of Judaism in Ḥimyar accelerated in the fifth and sixth centuries, with conversions reaching their apogee under the reign of Yusuf Dhu Nuwas (522–525). During his three years in power, he persecuted Christians, ordering the massacre of the Christian city of Najran in 523, for example, an event recorded in the annals and, commentators agree, alluded to by the Qurʾan (85:4). With the assistance of Byzantium, the Ethiopians two years later invaded Ḥimyar and toppled Dhu Nuwas. They appointed one of their own as leader (though he was immediately overthrown by another Ethiopian named Abraha), left a garrison, and returned to Ethiopia.

Evoking the reign of Justinian (527–565), or the period immediately preceding the coming of Muhammad, the Byzantine historian Procopius of Caesarea recounts these events and in passing reports that many Jews were present in southern Arabia:

> At about the time of this war Hellestheaeus, the king of the Aethiopians, who was a Christian and a most devoted adherent of this faith, discovered that a number of the Homeritae on the opposite mainland were oppressing the Christians there outrageously; many of these rascals were Jews and many of them held in reverence the old faith which men of the present day call Hellenic. He therefore collected a fleet of ships and an army and came against them and he conquered them in battle and slew both the king and many of the Homeritae. He then set up in his stead a Christian king, a Homerite by birth, by name Esimiphaeus, and, after ordaining that he should pay a tribute to the Aethiopians every year, he returned to his home.[5]

Between Arabia and the Holy Land

In addition to the Arab sources, archaeology also attests to these links between the kingdom of Ḥimyar and the Jews of Palestine. In the twentieth century, inscriptions were discovered concerning the Jews of Ḥimyar indicating that, long before the advent of Islam, there were in Arabia Jewish or Arab tribes that had converted to Judaism. To this day, the Ḥimyarite burial chamber, which dates from the third century CE and is located in the monumental necropolis of Beit She'arim, southeast of Mount Carmel, constitutes the oldest and most important archaeological discovery in this domain. In his book, *The Jews in Arabia (Israel ba-'Arav)*, H. Z. Hirschberg was the first to point out the great interest of these graves. In his view, the bodies of the deceased Ḥimyarites had not been transported two thousand kilometers from Ḥimyar; rather, members of this community had settled in one of the southeastern towns of the Holy Land.[6] Hirschberg's theories are supported by the recent discovery at Zoʻar to the south of the Dead Sea of inscriptions on Ḥimyarite Jewish tombs dating from 470 and 477 CE. They are written in a mix of Arabic, Aramaic, and Sabaean. One of them nevertheless indicates that the deceased had been transferred for burial at Zoʻar from Ḥimyar's capital Zafar (130 km south of Sanaʻa).

Hirschberg supposed that the majority of Jews—particularly those hailing from lands along the Via Odorifera, or incense road, far away from the historic centers of Palestine and Babylonia—were devoted to trade, a supposition confirmed by such literary sources as the pre-Islamic Arabic poetry of the sixth century. Among the Arab poets who mention Ḥimyarite Jews is Imruʼ al-Qays (ca. 500–550 CE), a prince from the kingdom of Kinda and vassal of Ḥimyar, who is said to have converted to Judaism in the pre-Islamic period.[7] The verses of other famous Arab poets state that the Jews of South Yemen produced and sold wine in the region of Ḥadhramawt. Indeed, amphoras of wine dating from the first century CE were recovered in underwater excavations at Qaniʼ (present-day Bʼir ʻAli), a town on the southern coast of Yemen.

Archeological studies teach us that the Jews of the kingdom of Ḥimyar were organized into a community possessing all of the usual institutions of the Jewish diaspora. The remnants of many synagogues have been found in the region, as have ritual baths.[8] The bath unearthed at Zafar by archeologists Paul Yule and Katharina Galor meets the ritual requirements of Jewish law (in its dimensions and form, and in the origin of its water) as stated in rabbinic sources.[9] Cemeteries exclusively reserved for Jews, in accordance with the requirements of law, have also been identified. Nevertheless, despite all of this archaeological evidence, it remains unknown what form of Judaism the Jews of Ḥimyar practiced: were they linked to the rabbinic Judaism of Palestine, or to that of Babylonia? Did they practice a more sectarian form of Judaism of a Judeo-Christian or proto-Karaite variety? The present state of research offers some possible leads (cf. Robin [ed.], *Le judaïsme de l'Arabie antique*), but it does not allow us to settle these questions definitively.

The Jewish Presence in the Hejaz in the Beginning of Islam

As we have just seen, Jews first began settling in the Hejaz centuries before the advent of Islam. They settled in Yathrib (the future Medina), as well as north of the town in the region of Wadi al-qura (the valley of villages), through which passed the ancient caravan route linking Yathrib to northwestern Arabia. This valley, roughly two hundred kilometers long, stretches from the Khaybar settlement, northeast of Yathrib, to Tayma' and the oasis of Fadak. By far the largest town of the region, Yathrib was situated to the northwest of a constellation of settlements—both towns and villages—interspersed with large open spaces, palm groves, fields and markets.

The Jews of Yathrib are said to have been distributed between three tribes: the Banu Nadir, the Banu Qurayza, and the Banu Qaynuqaʿ. Thanks to fertile land with many streams in Wadi al-qura and Yathrib, the Jews were heavily engaged in agriculture, cultivating vineyards and processing and exporting olives and, especially, dates. According to Michael Lecker, however, they drew their main subsistence from trade, not agriculture, as had their co-religionists in the kingdom of Ḥimyar: Yathrib's four pre-Islamic market places are evidence of particularly intense commercial activity. Inside the town, moreover, the tribes of Nadir and Qurayza possessed fortresses and fortified dwelling places that could never have been constructed solely with agricultural revenue. Many Jews, particularly those from the Qaynuqaʿ tribe, worked and traded silver. The three tribes also traded in weapons and armor.[10]

Muslim sources refer to the tribes of Nadir and Qurayza as *al-kahinan* (the two tribes of *Cohanim* or priests) or *Banu Harun* (sons of Aaron), for they claimed to descend from Moses' brother, the high priest Aaron. The *Cohanim* played an essential role in the life of the Temple and were subject to the strictest rules of purity, as is underscored in particularly detailed fashion in the Bible (Leviticus and Ezekiel, in particular) and subsequent Talmudic literature. In his book *Jews and Arabs*, Shlomo D. Goitein notes that, even centuries after the destruction of the Second Temple, towns uniquely populated by *Cohanim* were widespread. By means of these closed communities, the *Cohanim* sought to facilitate observance of their demanding rules of purity. Goitein concludes: "All this taken together leads us to accept the testimony of the Muslim writers that al-Medina, the main scene of Muhammad's activities, was originally a priestly town, a community of *Cohanim*, of which very considerable remnants were still extant in the Prophet's time."[11]

Goitein adds that, according to certain *midrashim* in the Talmud, the *Cohanim* chose to settle on the Arabian Peninsula after the destruction of the Second Temple. A Syriac text, *Ketaba de-Ḥimyaraya* (The Book of the Ḥimyarites), further indicates that *Cohanim* from Tiberias in the Holy Land were in the service of the king of Ḥimyar—undeniable evidence of the relationship between the Jews of Arabia and the Holy Land.[12]

This account perhaps settles the oft-debated question as to the ethnic origin of the Jews in Arabia: they were of Judean origin and not just converts, since a convert can never become *Cohen*. Nevertheless, it cannot be denied that there were also many converts to Judaism in Arabia, and all scholars fully agree that this was the case of the Jews of Ḥimyar.

The Qur'an and post-Qur'anic sources repeatedly refer to the influence of the Jews of Yathrib and its surroundings. The Qur'an very often mentions these *rabbaniyyun* (rabbis) and *aḥbar* (doctors) (Q. 5:44, as well as Q. 5:63 and Q. 9:31, 34). These Jewish sages read the Torah to the faithful and won their respect with their vast knowledge. Moreover, Jews and Christians are presented as the "people of the book" who made it possible for Muhammad to strengthen his faith: "If you are in doubt about what We send down to you, ask those who recited the Scripture before you" (Q. 10:94). It must be added that Muslim sources on many occasions mention the Jewish study house (*bayt al-midras* or, in Hebrew, *beit ha-midrash*) located in the lower town of Yathrib (*al-safila*), where a few of the town's pagans also studied. It is recounted that the women of Yathrib sent their children to grow up in Jewish families "for the Jews are men of knowledge and the Book."[13] Several *anṣar* ("helpers" of Muhammad, that is, Muslim natives of Yathrib) are said to have frequented these study houses, in particular Zayd b. Thabit, Muhammad's scribe and later head of the committee that the caliph 'Uthman (d. 656) appointed to establish the official text of the Qur'an, as the Tradition has it.[14] Yet we know almost nothing about the type of Judaism practiced by this community, that of Ḥimyar, or indeed the other communities of Arabia.

A question has often been debated among scholars of Islam: were the Jews of the pre-Islamic Hejaz Bedouins who spent their lives fighting, like the Arabs of the region? Or did they enjoy a peaceful life as town-dwellers and villagers? This question overlaps with that concerning the ethnic origin of the Jews. Having adopted the speculative views of the German Jewish historian Heinrich Graetz, Israel Friedlaender depicted the Jews of the Hejaz as nomads: "sons of the desert, men of the sword, soldiers, warriors."[15]

Hartwig Hirschfeld, for his part, held that there was no basis for this description and that it in no way corresponds to what is reported by the Muslim sources: the Jews were peaceful men, farmers, artisans and merchants inhabiting Yathrib and the neighboring towns to the north all along the Wadi al-qura. There may have been some warriors among them, but the majority of the population never took part in wars. The life of Jews in the region was not studded with acts of bravery.[16]

Which Judaism Did Muhammad Know in Arabia?

What holds for the Jews of the Hejaz holds for the Jews of Ḥimyar: no source tells us which form of Judaism they really practiced. Are we dealing with a homogenous religious group or a collection of currents or even sects whose practices and beliefs filtered their way into emergent Islam? The first reliable testimony to the existence of a Jewish community in the Hejaz practicing a form of Talmudic Judaism dates from the tenth century. It consists of fragments of Halakha questions addressed to the directors of Babylonian Talmudic academies (ge'onim), Rav Sherira Gaon (d. 1006) and Rav Hai Gaon (d. 1038), which were discovered in the Cairo Geniza. Two centuries later, the voyager Benjamin of Tudela (d. 1173) supplied another account along the same lines. These sources were written several centuries after the advent of Islam, however, and teach us nothing about the Jewish communities of the region in earlier periods.

The Qur'an itself in various places alludes to the fragmentation of opinion among Jews regarding the divine Scriptures that were revealed to them: "In the past, We gave Moses the Scripture but there was disagreement about it; and had it not been for a word that had preceded from your Lord, there would have been a decision between them; but they are in disquieting doubt about it" (Q. 11:110); and "This Qur'an recounts to the children of Israel most of that about which they differ" (Q. 27:76). Yet the accounts in the Qur'an are very general in tone. It is therefore difficult to draw precise conclusions regarding the Jewish currents and sects that had split from rabbinic Judaism on the Arabian Peninsula. This question has preoccupied many scholars, but despite a proliferation of theories, it remains very much a matter of uncertainty to this day.

Some think that the Qur'an alludes to the existence of a dominant, anti-Rabbinic current in Iraq and Persia in the first two centuries of Islam. Goitein, for his part, considers that the Judaism against which the Qur'an argues is a Karaite Judaism— or rather a proto-Karaite one, as Karaism only appeared well after the advent of Islam.[17] He thought that the Karaite imprint is *inter alia* evident in the respect shown the written Torah and the reservations expressed vis-à-vis post-biblical additions, which are denounced as "falsifications," an attitude similar to that of the Karaites. Other scholars such as Chaim Rabin in his article, "Islam and the Qumran Sect,"[18] and, in a more detailed way, Naphtali Wieder in his book *The Judean Scrolls and Karaism*, defend the view that the desert sects of Judea influenced Islam.

Another widely shared theory has it that the Qur'an echoes the Judeo-Christian conceptions of the Ebionites and even the Elcesaites, a late gnostic outgrowth of the former. A large body of recent research conceives of Qur'anic Judaism as a relic of Judeo-Christianity. This is the spirit of Holger Michael Zellentin's book *The Quar'ān's Legal Culture: The Didascalia Apostolorum as a Point of Departure*.[19] The author maintains that a significant majority of Qur'anic precepts and narrative episodes concerning the sons of Israel and Jesus echo those enunciated in the *Didascalia Apostolorum* and the pseudo-Clementine homilies. The *Didascalia Apostolorum*, a Jewish-accented Christian legal text, has partly survived in Greek, entirely in both Latin translation and a Syriac version produced after 683 CE. The pseudo-Clementine homilies, a fourth-century Judeo-Christian text written in Greek, have reached us in later Latin, Syriac, and Arabic versions. Although Zellentin takes care to specify that no relationship of direct interdependence exists between all these texts, and that this is particularly true of the *Didascalia* and the Qur'an, it is impossible not to be struck by their similarities. Indeed, he notes that the *Didascalia* and the Qur'an present a common point of view mingling faith and law. According to Zellentin, moreover, the legal portions of the Qur'an contained in the Medina suras cannot be uniquely explained by their relationship to such purely Jewish sources as the Talmud and that, among all the sources that influenced the Qur'an, the *Didascalia* remains the most salient. In the past, scholars have tended to explain the biblical elements of the Qur'an mainly by drawing comparisons with the Talmudic literature. Today, research into the Syriac Christian environment of the first Muslims is revealing other parallels. One may thus legitimately think of the writings of the Syriac Church Fathers, which precede the advent of Islam by several centuries, as sources for the Qur'an's biblical episodes. This point of view has been demonstrated, among others places, in the as yet unpublished dissertation of Joseph Witztum, "The Syriac Milieu of the Quran: The Recasting of the Biblical Narratives."[20]

Most of the aforementioned arguments are highly speculative, leaving the enigma of the sources of Qur'anic Judaism far from elucidated. Nor is it beside the point to recall that a handful of scholars tend to cast doubt on the very existence of Jewish communities in Arabia before the advent of Islam. There exists an entire "revisionist" or "hypercritical" school that, dismissing the Muslim sources a priori as belated constructions, proposes radical theories regarding the first decades of Islam. Moshe Sharon, one of the defenders of this "revisionist" thesis, thus holds that the Qur'an only appeared more than a half-century after Muhammad and thinks that Muslims only became aware of Jews and their religion following the conquest of Syria and Iraq, and that they then proceeded to describe the Jews of earlier periods on the model of their eighth and ninth century counterparts.[21] I shall not follow this line in the present book.

Arab Jewish Poets before Islam

Very little is known about the biographies of Jews living in the Hejaz before Islam arrived on the scene. One may nevertheless mention the best-known among them, the sixth-century CE poet al-Samaw'al (Shemu'el) b. 'Adiya', whose loyalty is praised in classical Arabic literature. The handful of his poems that have made their way to us leave much room for ambiguity. Thus, his most famous poem *lamiya* (a poem rhyming with the consonant "l") in no way differs from the poems of pagan Arabs. In it, al-Samaw'al praises the social and moral virtues of the pre-Islamic Arabs. Collectively known under the term *muruwwa* (virility), these virtues include protecting those in need, hospitality, and bravery in combat, among other qualities considered fundamental to Arab social morality, both before and after the advent of Islam. By contrast, the text of the poem makes no allusion to Jewish beliefs or elements originating in Jewish sources.

However, other poems were attributed to al-Samaw'al in which his Judaism is expressed via such biblical motifs as, for example, the prophesy regarding the kingdom of David. Yet these poems are of questionable authenticity, particularly the verses containing the allusions to the Bible, which do not figure in all versions of al-Samaw'al's *Diwan* (collected poems). Hirschberg examines at length a poem attributed to al-Samaw'al discovered in the Cairo Geniza[22] that contains many Jewish motifs. By contrast, the work of other Jewish poets from the pre-Islamic era that Muslims call Jahiliyya (the era of "ignorance") possesses this same pagan Arab character, lacking any obvious Jewish elements: that of Ka'b al-Aḥbar from the Qurayza tribe, for example, doubtless the most famous Jewish sage to convert to Islam at the time of Muhammad, or that of the obscure Jewish poetess Sarah, also from the Qurayza tribe. Another Jewish poetess from Yathrib, 'Aṣma,' daughter of Marwan, was to be assassinated by one of Muhammad's disciples after being accused of having written poems denigrating the Prophet of Islam.[23]

It must be noted, however, that all of our information concerning the Jews of Hejaz comes from Muslim sources, the better part of which were assembled long after the events they supposedly relate. In fact, these sources date from a period when Jewish communities no longer existed in most of the regions where they had formerly had a presence. In other words, we are confronted by a twofold methodological problem: first, the description of Jews and their religion entirely depends on external sources; second, none of these sources is contemporaneous with these Jewish communities. Dating from several centuries after the fact, they cannot be free of polemical overtones. They in fact describe the Jews as the Muslims perceived them after they had separated from and become hostile toward them. Some of the Prophet's helpers (*anṣar*) in Medina, known to harbor an affection for the Jews and even believed to have been influenced by them, were now held up to mockery. The terms applied to them—"Jew, son of Jew" and "Jewish sage (*ḥabr*)"— hardly seem laudatory.

In the absence of other sources, however, we are obliged to examine Muslim sources and, in particular, the Qur'an to get a sense of the contours of Judaism at the time of the advent of Islam and in the centuries that followed. And these sources are indeed replete with allusions to the Jews during the life of Muhammad, as well as in earlier periods. Goitein liked to remind us of the problem posed by these Muslim sources: the Qur'an, he wrote, "constitutes the sole source for research on the Jewish religion in Muhammad's entourage as well as the latter's attitude towards it."[24]

The Arabs and Palestine before Islam

At the same time, it is important to realize that, contrary to the romantic image of a Bedouin Arab people trapped in its desert, the pre-Islamic Arab world had extensive links with regions located northwest of the Arabian Peninsula properly so-called— with the lands they called *al-Sham*, which at the time consisted of the Byzantine provinces of Palestine, Phoenicia, and Syria. Among other accounts, Arab historians preserved traces of ancient accounts depicting Muhammad and his future follower 'Umar traveling in this region for trade, particularly to Gaza, before the Qur'anic revelation.

Pre-Islamic Arabs themselves distinguished between "Southern Arabs," seen as natives of the peninsula, and "Northern Arabs," a group that later claimed descent from Ismael and to which Muhammad's tribe, the Quraysh, belonged. At the time, moreover, there were two Arab kingdoms in the north of the peninsula: that of the Ghassanids, vassals of the Byzantines in southern Syria, and that of the Lakhmids, vassals of the Persians in southern Mesopotamia.[25]

The Arabic language itself, so inseparable from the Qur'an, bears traces of this civilization's situation, located midway between the Syro-Palestinian world and that of Southern Arabia. Before the Qur'an, it is true, Arabic was the language of the Bedouins, but it was also that of the Arab kingdoms mentioned above. It belongs to the same sub-family of Semitic languages as Hebrew and Aramaic, while the Southern Arabian languages belong to a rather distant branch in the same group as the Ethiopian languages. What's more, the Arabic in which the Qur'an was written has many more Hebrew and Aramaic influences than does classical Arabic.

The First Muslim Community and the Jews of Medina

The *hijra*, which marks the start of the Islamic calendar commemorates Muhammad's flight to Yathrib in 622, fleeing the persecution to which he and his small circle of followers had been subjected in Mecca. Here, he found well-established Jewish communities, and it was in Yathrib, which would later be known as Medina (or, in Arabic, *al-Madina*, "the City", an exact equivalent of the word *medina* in post-biblical Hebrew), that the first Islamic state was constructed and that Muhammad established himself, not just as a religious preacher, but also as a political leader. One of the founding gestures of this political *islam*, in the etymological sense of "pacification," consisted in establishing the Prophet as the "judge of peace" who would resolve any conflicts that might arise between the various components of Medina society: the Meccan Muslims who had "emigrated" to Medina, known as *Muhajirun*; the Aws and Khazraj, Medina Arab tribes that converted to Islam and were called "helpers" (*al-anṣar*); and the largest Jewish tribes, the Qurayza, Qaynuqaʿ, and Nadir (as well as others, such as the ʿAwf). These groups were bound together by a "Pact of Mutual Understanding and Support" that would subsequently be known as the "Medina Constitution." Among other measures, this held that the Jewish tribes "formed, with the Believers [i.e., the Muslims], a single community, *umma*."

The years 622–632 were decisive for the construction of Islam and have served as a symbolic point of reference throughout Muslim history. Over the course of this decade, Muhammad built a state, created a Muslim society, and waged several decisive battles against his Meccan adversaries: the battles of Badr (624), Uḥud (625), and that known as "the Trench" (*al-khandaq*) (627). Muslim tradition recounts that, on each of these three occasions, one of the Jewish tribes broke the mutual assistance pact and betrayed the Prophet, thereby justifying the reprisals against them. During the Battle of the Trench, the Qurayza, in particular, were accused of trying to attack the Medina armies from the rear. Muhammad put their fate into the hands of their former allies, the Aws, who judged them "in keeping with the rules of war as codified in the Torah": pubescent males were executed and the women and children were reduced to bondage.[26]

The degradation of relations between Jews and Muslims in Medina is mentioned in the Qurʾan by way of allusions to the setbacks suffered by the Jewish tribes. While none of the three great Jewish tribes living in Medina and its surroundings is explicitly named in the Qur'an, the exegetical tradition nevertheless agrees that various verses allude to them. One verse, for example, reads: "Many of the People of the Scripture want to make you unbelievers again after you have believed, through envy on their part after the truth has become clear to them. . . ." (Q. 2:109). Or, as the first lines of sura 59 have it: "[It is] He who has driven those of the People of the Scripture who have disbelieved from their dwellings for the first rounding up. You did not think that they would leave and they thought that their strongholds would defend them against God. But God reached them from a place they did not reckon on. . . ." (Q. 59:2). These verses are understood by many Muslim commentators as recounting the expulsion and exile of the Nadir tribe. For Muslim exegetes, the same sura subsequently alludes to the fate of the Qaynuqaʿ tribe with these lines: "like those who, shortly before them, tasted the mischief of their affair. They will have painful torment" (Q. 59:15).

In various Qur'anic verses, Muslim commentators also perceive episodes from the life of the Qurayza tribe prior to its final destruction. Thus, sura 8 is devoted to the description of the trophies of war taken following the battle of Badr, marking the Muslims' victory over the Meccan polytheists. According to the exegetes, however, it also justifies the war against the Qurayza on the grounds that they had betrayed their alliance with the Prophet: "Those of them with whom you [Muhammad] have made a Covenant and then they break their Covenant every time and do not protect themselves" (Q. 8:56). Verse 26 of sura 33 recounts how Muhammad expelled the members of the tribe from their small forts and, in verses Q. 33:60–61, the preparations taken for waging war against them are mentioned: "Accursed, and they will be seized wherever they are found and will be slaughtered" (Q. 33:61). Yet the Qur'an does not describe the massacres to which they were subjected and only briefly alludes to the fate of the Medina Jews. This is in contrast to Muslim historic literature and works of *Sira* ("biographies" of the Prophet), such as the well-known *Sira* by Muhammad Ibn Isḥaq (d. 768), revised by ʿAbd al-Malik Ibn Hisham (d. 834), which offer detailed accounts of their expulsion and forced exile, especially of the massacre of the Qurayza tribe.[27]

The last great battle between Muhammad and the Jewish tribes was that of Khaybar in 628, which took place shortly before the capture of Mecca. Located 150 kilometers north of Medina, Khaybar was mainly populated by Jews. The Muslim armies attacked the town in reprisal for the betrayal of the Banu Nadir, who were associated with it. The town was taken, but its inhabitants were not massacred, instead becoming the first group to be subjected to the payment of *jizya*, the tax on conquered non-Muslim populations. In 642, ten years after the death of Muhammad, his successor, ʿUmar ibn al-Khattab, deported the Jews of Khaybar to Syria as part of the general expulsion of non-Muslims from the Hejaz. This expulsion was doubtless more a matter of ideology than of fact, however, for in the twelfth century, the Jewish traveler Benjamin of Tudela claimed to have encountered Jewish communities still living in Khaybar and Taymaʾ. In the Muslim imaginary, Khaybar nevertheless became synonymous with the Prophet's last battle against the Jews, a notion that was to be revived by the anti-Jewish Islamist discourse of the twenty-first century.

Though an essential part of Muslim memory, these episodes are unknown to Jewish tradition, which has nothing to say about Jewish communities on the Arabian Peninsula. To this day, the asymmetric memory of the Jewish and Muslim traditions in this respect is the source of much misunderstanding.

II

The Representation of Judaism
and Jews in the Qur'an

THE QUR'AN presents itself to us as a book divided into chapters known as "suras," which consist of a variable number of verses. In contrast to the Torah and other biblical books, however, it does not read as a narrative. The order of the suras is arbitrary, seemingly organized on the basis of the length of the chapters, from longer to shorter, rather than in any kind of chronological or thematic order. For almost the entire prophetic mission of Muhammad, the Qur'an consisted of an assortment of verses or disparate groups of verses revealed according to circumstances. According to Muslim tradition, it was only in the final months of his life that Muhammad ordered them to be gathered together. All of this renders the work of interpreting the Qur'an difficult. While certain sura—the twelfth, for example, or *Yusuf* (Joseph)—can be read as narrative, many of them, such as the third, *Al 'Imran* [The Family of 'Imran], at first reading appear unfocused. For this reason, the specific manner in which verses are interpreted depends less on their place in the sura than on the original circumstances in which they were revealed (*asbab al-nuzul*), circumstances that the Qur'an itself does not indicate and that commentators attempt to reconstruct on the basis of oral tradition.

At the end of the previous chapter, I mentioned the *hijra*, Muhammad's emigration to Medina. This episode marks an invisible caesura in the Qur'an itself, which both contemporary scholars and classical commentators believe separates the "Meccan" from the "Medinan" sura and verses. The former, received in the period when Muhammad, nearly alone, was preaching to an indifferent and sometimes hostile crowd, are mainly eschatological and moral in tenor; the latter, set forth in the sociopolitical context of an emergent and soon-to-be triumphant Islam, give prominent place to legal prescriptions and polemics against Jews, Christians, and other groups that declined to join the nascent Muslim community.

The Various Names Given the Jews in the Qur'an

The Qur'an employs three distinct terms to refer to the Jews, each of which places the emphasis on a different aspect. Most often *banu Isra'il* (children of Israel), denotes the descendants of Israel in the biblical period, though it is also used, albeit infrequently, to refer to Muhammad's Jewish contemporaries. Sometimes, it is highly favorable: the children of Israel are the chosen people (Q. 2:47 and Q. 2:122) whom God freed from servitude by leading them out of Egypt and into the Holy Land (Q. 5:21). But the expression also can be pejorative, as when the children of Israel break their alliance with God (Q. 5:13) by prostrating themselves before the golden calf. The Hebrews are also referred to as children of Israel" when they are accused of killing the prophets.[1] In most cases, however, the term seems ambivalent in its import.

The term *al-yahud* (the Jews) and the locution *alladhina hadu* (those who became Jews / those who practice Judaism) generally refer to Jews of the post-biblical periods, above all to the Jews known to Muhammad in Mecca and Medina. Here the terms most often carry a pejorative connotation. Those accused of having falsified the Torah, for example, are described as "Jews" (Q. 4:46). Those who believed, like Christians, that God sired a son named 'Uzayr (Q. 9:30) are also referred to as "Jews."[2] Obviously, the Qur'an cautions, one must be wary of entering into alliance with them, just as one should keep one's distance from Christians (Q. 5:51).

The third expression, *ahl al-kitab* (the people of the book), does not refer solely to Jews, but also to Christians who are in possession of the revealed sacred Scriptures. The Qur'an mainly references the Bible in two ways: as *al-Kitab* (the Book) and as *al-Tawrat*, a term that refers, beyond the Torah (or Pentateuch) in the strict sense, to the Hebrew Bible in its entirety, and sometimes even encompasses post-biblical Jewish sources. The text of the Qur'an also mentions *al-Zabur* (that is, the Book of Psalms) as an independent holy book revealed to David: "... We preferred some of the prophets over others and We gave psalms [*al-Zabur*] to David" (Q. 17:55). The Qur'an also makes vague mentions of what are called "the scrolls of Abraham and Moses" (*suhuf Ibrahim wa-Musa*, Q. 87:19) or simply "the former Scriptures" (*al-suhuf al-ula*, Q. 20:133).[3] It is not known which specific scriptures are meant here: perhaps the expression simply refers to statements by these two prophets (and others) mentioned in the Qur'an.

Alongside these terms used of the ancient Hebrews and the Jews contemporaneous with Muhammad, are various others. Sometimes they are referred to as *kafirun* (plural of *kafir*, "unbeliever"). There are also Qur'anic verses that mention the divine wrath directed against "sinners," which according to the commentators often refer to Jews and Christians. This is the case, for example, of the verse with which the first sura of the Qur'an (*al-fatiḥa*) concludes: "Guide us on the straight path. The path of those You have blessed, not of those against whom there is anger nor of those who go astray" (Q. 1:6–7). As one can see, the Qur'an expresses itself here in rather general terms, without direct reference to specific groups. From the earliest commentaries, however, it is quite clear that "those You have blessed" are the first Muslims, whereas "[those] against whom there is anger" are the Jews, and "those who go astray" are the Christians. It is in these terms, for example, that they are described by Tabari (d. 923), one of the Qur'an's greatest exegetes.

The Children of Israel, a Chosen People

The image of Jews and Judaism that emerges from the Qur'an varies according to whether those meant are the biblical Hebrews or the contemporaries of Muhammad. The verses in which God lavishes his praise on the children of Israel may be divided into three categories: those that portray the children of Israel as chosen people; those that relate to the exodus from Egypt and arrival in the Promised Land; and those that speak of the Alliance with God and the giving of the Torah, seen as a source confirming Islam. As we shall see below, these positive assessments require some qualification.

The idea of Israel's election frequently recurs in the Qur'an. Sometimes it touches the entire people, in other instances only a few figures or families, such as those of Abraham, 'Imran (that is, 'Amram, father of Aaron, Moses and Myriam), and certain prophets. The idea is expressed by a series of closely related verbs like *iṣtafa, faddala, ijtaba,* and *ikhtara* or, as in the Bible, without any particular terminology. In some verses, election emerges on its own from the grace God showed Israel and the many benefits He lavished upon them: "In the past We gave the Children of Israel the Scripture (*al-kitab*) and the Judgment (*al-ḥukm*) and the Prophethood (*al-nubuwwa*) and We provided them with good things and preferred them over all created beings" (Q. 45:16). Or, as another verse has it: "O my people, remember all the blessings of God to you when he placed prophets amongst you and made you kings and gave you what He had not given to any one [else] among created beings" (Q. 5:20).

In the first verse, election is expressed by the verb *faddala*, which means "to prefer": the children of Israel are "preferred" over other peoples or "raised" above them. In the second verse, by contrast, the vocabulary of election is absent and the idea emerges that Israel received favors not accorded to other peoples.

The idea of election nearly always occurs in a polemical context and sometimes even serves as the point of departure for such a discussion. As one might expect, it is also encountered in connection with other subjects of disagreement between Islam and its rival sister religions, Judaism and Christianity. Several verses present the idea of election as a "historical" fact. We see this in sura 2 verse 47, for example, and again in verse 122: "Children of Israel, remember my blessings which I bestowed on you and how I favored you over [all] created beings." The polemical dimension in these two verses (47 and 122) is quite marked. An entire series of historical reminders intervenes between the two. Following the first verse, the exodus from Egypt, the crossing of the Red Sea with dry feet, and Pharaoh's drowning and its consequences are all cited (a few verses even mention his entire army, for example Q. 44:24: "they are a drowned host"). Alongside this are several miracles described in the Bible, most of them having taken place as the Children

of Israel wandered the desert: the manna and quails that fell
from the sky (Q. 2:57; Q. 7:160) and the twelve springs that appeared when the people complained to Moses of the lack of
water (Q. 2:60). There is also an allusion to God's meetings with
Moses during the forty nights the people used to build the
golden calf (Q. 2:51). One also finds a reference to the revelation
on Mt. Sinai (Q. 2:63), the red heifer (Q. 2:67–73),[4] and others.

The impression that clearly emerges from these Qur'an passages is that Israel's election is *conditional* in nature: from their
exodus from Egypt to their entry into "the Holy Land which
God has prescribed for you" (Q. 5:21), the people seem vindic-
tive and ungrateful, a representation that is moreover consistent
with their depiction in the books of Exodus and Numbers. Yet,
in contrast to the Mosaic text and the books of the prophets,
which constantly reiterate that the various divine punishments
visited upon Israel do not call into question God's uncondi-
tional fidelity to it, in the Qur'an the people's conduct justifies
that they be stripped of election. Indeed, reminders of their
election and of the divine favors associated with it are an occasion for rebuke. The prevailing tone is one of reprimand. This
is expressed with particular vehemence in the passages that
follow the two verses mentioned above: "Protect yourselves
against a day when no soul will give any satisfaction for any
other nor will any intercession be accepted from it nor any
equivalent taken from it and they will not be helped" (Q. 2:48;
cf. also Q. 2:123).

This warning may be—and in fact was—interpreted as putting the faithful on notice that election was not guaranteed once
and for all. Quite the contrary, it could be given over to others,
in particular to Muslims: "So that the People of the Book know
that they can in no way do without the grace of God. Yes, grace
is in the hands of God; He gives it to whomever he wishes. God

is the Master of boundless Grace" (Q. 57:29). The word translated here as "grace," *fadl*, can also include the notion of election.[5] This idea was extensively developed by many commentators in regards to the verse, "We chose them through knowledge (*ikhtarnahum 'ala 'ilm*) above created beings" (Q. 44:32). Significantly, it is the concept of election that here brings the account of the exodus from Egypt to its conclusion. It is even stated that divine choice acts "through knowledge" (*'ala 'ilm*). Election nevertheless remains a temporary and conditional gift.

Tabari refines this idea of conditional election. In his view, the circumstances that justified Israel's election—to wit, the existence of numerous prophets in its midst—no longer held. To this, he adds another argument drawn from the exegetical tradition, which he cites in connection with verse Q. 2:47: "This idea (that is, the election of the Children of Israel) depends on their observance of God's commandments. But some of them were punished (they were transformed into monkeys)[6] and they became the foulest of creatures and it was to Muslims that God said: 'You are the best community brought forth for the people'" (Q. 3:110).[7]

Tabari's exegesis justifying the transfer of election away from Israel by virtue of its sins is also familiar from Christian polemics against the Jews, for Christianity, too, explained God's abandonment of Israel as a result of the people's sins. As its replacement, God chose "the remnant of Israel"[8]—that is, the Christians, those who followed Jesus and represented the *Verus Israel*,[9] or "true Israel." The Muslim attitude does not differ fundamentally from the Christian position. It is a recurrent idea in the Qur'an and is particularly characteristic of the Shi'i vision, as we shall see in the final chapter.

The Qur'an's praise for the children of Israel must thus be set in a broader context in which the election of the people of Israel is clearly an ambiguous notion. The following verse, for example, which takes a particularly polemical stance toward the Jews and Christians, contests and in fact rejects the idea of election:

> The Jews and the Christians say: 'We are the children of God, the ones He loves.' Say: "Then, why does He punish you for your sins?" No. You are mortals, of those He has created. He forgives those whom He wishes and punishes those whom He wishes. God has sovereignty over the heavens and the earth and what is between them. To Him is the journeying. (Q. 5:18).

In his article, "The Idea of Election in Early Islam," Haggai Ben-Shammai makes two observations regarding this verse. First, he notes that it contains an explicit polemic against any literal notion of election as it is encountered in Judaism and the Christian interpretation thereof. Historical experience proves that this election is obsolete, for election or particular proximity to God depends on divine will. Second, he observes that, though the claim attributed to the Jews by this Qur'anic verse relies on a few biblical verses and perhaps some liturgical expressions coined at the time of the Mishna and Talmud, it also attributes it to the Christians. The Qur'an here reflects an old argument against the Jews already voiced by first century Christians, according to which the historical situation of the Jews invalidates their claim to election.[10]

Yet it must nevertheless be acknowledged that, for the sake of consistency, the Qur'an commentators also present the moral behavior of Muslims as a condition of their election. Commenting upon the verse, "You are the best community brought forth for the people" (Q. 3:110), Tabari reminds us that the verse continues as follows: "You enjoin what is reputable and you forbid the disreputable and you believe in God." These words may be interpreted as referring to the Muslim community (or nation, *umma*) in general, but also, according to certain traditional exegeses quoted by Tabari, as a statement of the terms of valid election. In other words, their election only operates if the Muslim *umma* observes what God ordains in this verse ("enjoining what is reputable and forbidding the disreputable and believing in God"). Election is therefore not an eternal state of grace that can be taken for granted.[11] The behavior of the people or of individuals and groups within it may grant them election or deprive them of it.

In Shiʿi Islam, what's more, there is a tendency to attribute election, not to all Muslims, but solely to the Shiʿa—that is, those who recognize the Imams as the only legitimate heirs of Muhammad. The famous Shiʿi exegete ʿAli b. Ibrahim al-Qummi (late ninth–early tenth century) thus claimed that this verse cannot be applied to all Muslims, since there are among the latter notorious sinners whose crimes include the assassination of Imams. The verse may be applied only to a select group: the Shiʿi Imams themselves, seen as totally free of sin. In support of this exegesis, Shiʿi tradition imposes an alternate reading of verse Q. 3:110: not "You are the best community (*umma*)," but rather "you are the best Imams (*aʾimma*) brought forth for the people."[12]

The critique that Sunni Islam levels against other religions is accordingly adopted within Islam itself by the Shiʿa and turned against the Sunnis. It is not only the Jews who are not an elected people. Election is exclusive: its only beneficiaries are a small community of the chosen within Shiʿism or, at most, all Shiʿa.

God's Covenant with the People of Israel

In the Qurʾan, one also finds echoes of biblical passages that speak of God's Covenant with the people of Israel, a mark of their election. Referred to in the Qurʾan as *mithaq* or *ʿahd*, this Covenant is a central component of the historic role attributed by God to Israel. It is the story of a promise in several steps: liberation from bondage; divine choice; the establishment of the Covenant; and guidance to the Promised Land and the tribes' settlement there. Just like election, the Covenant is a synallagmatic contract between God and the chosen people:

> Children of Israel! [. . .]. Fulfill [your] Covenant with Me and I shall fulfill [My] Covenant with you, and fear Me. And believe in what I have sent down, confirming what is with you, and do not be the first to disbelieve in it; and do not sell My signs for a small price, and fear Me. Do not confuse falsehood with truth and do not conceal the truth knowingly. (Q. 2:40–42).

The Covenant in question here and in other verses is that concluded between the Children of Israel and God after their exodus from Egypt. At that time, God drew "twelve leaders" (*naqibs*; Q. 5:12) from among them—a number that corresponds, it seems, to the leaders of the twelve tribes of Israel (Numbers 7:2)—and sent them prophets (Q. 5:70). The Covenant was agreed upon, it is claimed, at Mount Sinai, but this placename is not mentioned. In the verse, one only finds the Aramaic loan-word *tur* (mountain): "And [recall] when We took your Covenant from you and raised the mountain (*al-tur*) above you: 'Take firm hold of what We have given you [. . .]'" (Q. 2:63).

This image of God raising the mountain over the head of the children of Israel gathered at its foot, like the claim that they must accept the Torah with a "firm hold" (*bi-quwwa*), recurs elsewhere in the Qur'an.[13] As many scholars have underscored, there is a clear parallel with a famous *midrash* found, among other places, in the Babylonian Talmud:

> "And they stood at the lowermost part of the mountain" (Ex. 19:17): The Holy One, Blessed be He, overturned the

mountain above [them] like a tub and said to them: "If you accept the Torah, excellent, if not, there will be your burial" (*Babylonian Talmud, Shabbat* 88a).[14]

The reference in the Qur'an is very vague but certain exegetes elaborate upon it in line with this midrash.[15] Associated with election, the divine Covenant is also a form of conditional grace. From the outset, it was accompanied by a series of warnings: "Do not be the first to disbelieve in it; and do not sell My signs for a small price" (Q. 2:41). Since every mention of the Covenant is accompanied by a reminder of its violation, the Qur'an leaves its readers in no doubt as to its having been concluded with a people destined to break it. For example, following the exodus from Egypt, when God demanded that the children of Israel serve Him alone, that they treat their parents, loved ones and orphans with respect and compassion, and that they not shed innocent blood or drive away those who live among them, it is immediately noted that the Children of Israel failed to live up to these moral demands and, "apart from a few of you" (Q. 2:83), turned their backs on them. To this, the Qur'an adds these harsh words:

"There you were, killing one another and expelling a group of you from their dwellings, supporting one another against them in sin and enmity . . ." (Q. 2:85).

In these verses, there is no reference whatsoever to the context. If the reference is to a historical reality, it is impossible to say which. When did the Hebrews drive out people living among them? But while the Qur'an says nothing, its exegesis sheds light on the matter: according to some commentators, this obscure verse does not refer to the biblical period but rather to the Nadir and Qurayza, the two Jewish tribes living in Yathrib whose alliance with the local Arab tribes, the Aws and

Khazraj, predated Islam.[16] When the latter went to war with one another, each of the two Jewish tribes had to rush to the aid of their Arab allies and in this way found themselves involved in a fratricidal struggle. As soon as Muhammad had consolidated his power in Medina, he turned against them at great cost to them.[17]

This exegetical approach is a good example of how the Qur'anic message was brought up to date: verses that describe the Hebrews' struggle against their enemies in the biblical period—in this instance, Pharaoh and his army—are associated with Muhammad's struggle against the Jewish tribes of Medina and its surroundings.

From Egypt to the Holy Land

In keeping with the Bible, the Qur'an presents Israel's election and its Covenant with God as the two foundations of the lofty status attributed to the people of Israel. God's love for them is expressed by the protection he accords them under Pharaoh's yoke and the plagues of Egypt and by his the liberation of the Hebrews. These subjects are all mentioned on several occasions in the Qur'an, for example in Q. 7:103–162; Q. 26:10–67 and Q. 28:6–41. The gift of land is presented as the fulfillment of this divine promise: "And We caused the people who had been thought weak to inherit the eastern and western parts of the land, on which We had bestowed blessings. And the fairest Word (*kalima*)[18] of your Lord was fulfilled for the Children of Israel in return for their patience . . ." (Q. 7:137).

Echoing the Book of Numbers and that of Joshua, various passages also mention the conquest of Canaan and the settling of the territory that the Qur'an describes as the "Holy Land" (*al-ard al-muqaddasa*):

And [recall] when Moses said to his people, "O my people, remember the blessings of God to you when He placed prophets amongst you and made you kings and gave you what He had not given to any one [else] among created beings. O my people, enter the Holy Land which God had prescribed for you. Do not turn your backs, lest you return as losers". They said, "Moses, there is in it a people who are men of might. We shall not enter it until they leave it. If they leave it, we shall enter." Then two men whom God had blessed from among those who feared [God] said, "Go through the gate into their presence. If you enter through it, you will be victorious. Put your trust [in God] if you are believers." They said: "Moses, we shall never enter it as long as they are in it! Go with your Lord and the two of you fight [them]. We shall sit here" (Q. 5:20–24).

As elsewhere, the verses quoted here mingle praise with disapproval. There is a positive judgment, reflecting the fact that the people of Israel were the source of prophets and kings and for this reason deserved to conquer the land intended for them. But there is disapproval as well, due to their rebellion and lack of faith, as expressed in their discussions with Moses. In the group of explorers sent to inspect the country, two figures stand out. The Qur'an, like the Bible, describes both as men of faith. As is often the case in the Qur'an (see below, Chapter 3), their names are not mentioned. Yet readers familiar with the Torah will have little difficulty identifying these anonymous figures as the heroes of this biblical episode, Joshua, son of Nun, and Caleb, son of Jephunneh (Numbers 13–14).

A few centuries after Muhammad, the classical commentators of the Qur'an nevertheless found it difficult to identify this "holy land." Some believed it referred to "Mount Sinai and its

surroundings," others to "Al-Sham"—that is, Syria-Palestine—
others to "Jericho," yet others to "Damascus and Palestine".[19]
In other passages concerning the conquest of Canaan, God
orders the Hebrews to enter an unnamed town: "Enter this
settlement and eat plentifully from it wherever you wish; but
enter [through] the gate in prostration and say 'an unburden-
ing'" (Q. 2:58). Here, too, Qur'anic exegetes suggested that this
should be identified with Jerusalem or Jericho. Sometimes the
text confines itself to mentioning the town gate through which
the people will enter (Q. 4:154).

The Torah as Confirmation of the Qur'an

This reminder of the divine advantages conferred upon the
people of Israel elicits positive declarations as to their wisdom,
their prophets and, of course, the heaven-sent gift of the Torah,
which shall be discussed further below. In any case, the Qur'an's
attitude towards the Jews (and Christians) remains complex: although it is suspicious of the Holy Scriptures in their possession,
the Qur'an considers them as validating its own message. This
point of view is clearly expressed in the verse cited above: "If you
are in doubt about what We send down to you, ask those who
recited the Scripture before you" (Q. 10:94). According to the
usual interpretation, this verse is addressed to the Prophet in
order to show him that, should he be in any doubt as to the
Revelation he has received, he can always consult the People of
the Book—that is, the Jews and Christians. What they will
teach him on the basis of their Scriptures will help him
strengthen his own prophesy: "And those who take their stand
on a clear proof from their Lord when a witness from Him re-
cites it (and before it [there was] the Scripture of Moses as an
example and a mercy)—those believe in it" (Q. 11:17). What's

more, the Qur'an presents the Scriptures of the Jews and Christians as containing references to Muhammad and the principles of the religion heralded by him: "... The prophet of his community, whom they will find mentioned in the Torah and the Gospel" (Q. 7:157).

Although this brief overview is far from exhausting all of the Qur'an's positive statements regarding the Jews and their religion, it gives an idea of what aspects were singled out by the text and its exegeses. For all that, one must not overlook the negative judgements also to be found there.

Unruly and Rebellious Children

The severe criticism leveled by the Qur'an against the Hebrews of the Bible, and then against the Jews of later generations, occupies a larger place than do its positive judgements. They are "unruly and rebellious children," "transgressors of the divine Covenant" and, alongside other crimes of idolatry, worshippers of the golden calf. They falsified the Torah, killed their prophets, engaged in usury, and the list goes on.

The Qur'an adopts the biblical depiction of the Hebrews exiting Egypt as rebellious, sinful, and ungrateful. Although God had freed them from slavery, led them to the Promised Land, and concluded a Covenant with them, the Hebrews were said to have responded to Him as he prepared to give them the Torah: *sami'na wa-'asayna* ("We hear and disobey") (Q. 2:93). Here, one recognizes an echo of the famous response: "We will hear it and do it," *we-shama'nu we-'asinu* (Deuteronomy 5:7). But the Qur'an plays upon these words, transforming *'asinu* ("we shall do") into *'asayna* ("we shall disobey"), simply replacing the s/س/שׁ with the similar-sounding ṣ/ص/צ. This, however, inverts the meaning and is doubtless one reason why the

Qur'an accuses the Hebrews of having intentionally modified the divine message.

In the heat of the polemic, the Hebrews' breaking of the Covenant is transposed to Jewish history as a whole: "The worst of beasts in God's view are the ungrateful ones who do not believe, those of them with whom you have made Covenant and then they break their Covenant every time . . ." (Q. 8:55–56). These remarks are offered in general terms without reference to specific individuals or groups. And yet it must be noted that most classical commentators, in keeping with their usual method of reconstructing the context of Qur'anic verses, see them not as criticism targeting sinners or Jews in general, but rather as a quite specific attack against the Jews, the members of one or another of the Medina tribes mentioned above.[20]

This is a very important point: no text, to say nothing of an oft-difficult text like the Qur'an, lends itself to an absolute reading. The meaning that one takes from it heavily depends on the context one assigns to its verses. Taken in isolation, some highly polemical sentences are thus "neutralized" when understood in a specific historical context; conversely, verses can become "explosive" when they are intentionally decontextualized so as to be brandished against the Jews and Christians of our day. When they call for the "suppression" or "theological obsolescence" of certain verses of the Qur'an, anti-Muslim polemicists are in reality playing into the hands of Islamists by lending credibility to the idea that the Qur'an has a single clear meaning.

Idolators and Worshippers of the Golden Calf

The Hebrews' breaking of the Covenant is a broad accusation, and the various sins in which it resulted are ticked off like a litany: refusal of the signs sent by God, falsification of the words revealed to the prophets, and the killing of the prophets, among others. But the gravest offense is idolatry, tangible proof of the Hebrews' and then the Jews' rejection of monotheism. They fabricated and then worshipped the golden calf, and for this God threatened to exterminate the infidel people (Exodus 32:10). The Qur'an revisits this episode time and again as the worst possible sin:

> [God] said, "We have tempted your people after you left them and al-Samiri has led them astray." So Moses returned to his people, angry and sorry. He said, "My people, did your Lord not make you a fair promise, did the period of the Covenant last too long for you or did you want anger from your Lord to descend on you and so you failed [to keep] your tryst with me?" They said, "We did not fail [to keep] our tryst with you on our own free will but we were loaded with burdens of the ornaments of the people and so we threw them into the fire, as al-Samiri did." Then he produced for them a calf, a body that could make a lowing sound. They said, "this is your god and the god of Moses but he has forgotten . . ." (Q. 20:85–88)

This Qur'anic account in many respects resembles the biblical episode of the golden calf (Exodus 32:1–6). Its particularity resides in the intervention of the "Samaritan" (*al-Samiri*), which is absent from the biblical text. The Samaritans, who took their name from the town of Samaria and its region, located between Judea and Galilee, were a rival people to the Jews. Today nearly completely vanished, they claim to be the authentic descendants of the people of Israel. They recognize only the Torah, which they write in their own alphabet derived from the ancient Hebrew alphabet, and claim that God chose Mount Gerizim rather than Jerusalem for the site of his Temple. The Jews, for their part, consider them foreign imposters imported into the Holy Land by the Assyrians. Prior to that, the kingdom of Israel had been divided, following the reign of Solomon, into two kingdoms, that of Judea and that of the North, with its capital at Shechem (traditionally identified with the present-day town of Nablus). The book of Kings recounts that, in order to divert pilgrims away from Jerusalem, the King of the North, Jeroboam, introduced two golden calves for worship by the faithful. The rivalry between the Jews and the Samaritans is post-biblical since it mainly played out between the return of the captives from Babylonia and the era of the Hasmoneans. In a note to his translation of the Qur'an, Régis Blachère cites Ignác Goldziher to the effect that "this episode of the Samaritan establishing the cult of the golden calf was intended, as Goldziher has clearly showed, to situate the origin of the schism that took place between the Samaritan and Israelite communities in an ancient sin."[21]

Whatever the case, the episode of the golden calf serves to underscore the Hebrews' idolatry and call into question their commitment to monotheism.

The Figure of 'Uzayr

The other grave accusation of idolatry levelled against the people of Israel is found in a famous verse where they are represented as worshipping a certain 'Uzayr, who they believed to be the son of God:

> The Jews say, "'Uzayr is the son of God" and the Christians say: "Christ is the son of God." That is what they say in their mouths, conforming to what was said by those who disbelieved before them. God confound them. How they are embroiled in lies! (Q. 9:30)

What does the name 'Uzayr mean? Among scholars of the Qur'an, some suggest that it is a deformation of the biblical word '*Azazel* (Leviticus 16:8–10, which probably refers to a demon) or of the name of the Egyptian divinity Osiris. However, the most commonly accepted opinion among Muslim authors is that 'Uzayr is an Arabic diminutive of the name of Ezra or Esdras. In Muslim tradition, '*Uzayr al-warraq* is an exact translation of "Ezra the scribe" (in Hebrew: '*Ezra ha-sofer*), as he is called in the Bible (Nehemiah 12:36) and in post-biblical Jewish sources.[22] Whether the Qur'anic appellation refers to the biblical Ezra or some other figure, no Jewish source corroborates the Qur'an's accusation that the Jews had taken 'Uzayr for the son of God. In this respect, this calumny differs from many other polemical accusations in having no precedent in pre-Islamic anti-Jewish literature. In general, the fact that this argument should be put forward in the Qur'an alongside the Christian belief in the divine filiation of Jesus underscores the verse's polemical intent to present Judaism and Christianity alike as corrupted monotheisms. Juxtaposing this verse with the polemical verses directed against Judaism and Christianity only further underscores its polemical character.

As Newby suggested in his study of the history of Jews in Arabia in the pre-Islamic period, however, it is possible that the origin of this belief is in the identification of the figure of 'Uzayr with that of Enoch, of whom the Bible says: "And Enoch walked with God; and he *was* not; for God took him" (Genesis 5:24). The strange fate of Enoch, mysteriously taken away like Elijah (II Kings 2:11), gave him a special place in Jewish tradition. Post-biblical Jewish literature—and this is true of what are known as the "apocryphal" texts as well as mystical ones (the *First, Second,* and *Third Books of Enoch*)—attests to the belief that Enoch had been taken away to heaven while still alive, where he was transformed into an archangel named Metatron. Among other deeds, this Metatron, a quasi-divine figure (who some texts call "the little YHWH"), is said to have been the figure who dictated the Torah to Moses at Sinai. Newby claims that, among the Jews of Arabia, some saw 'Uzayr/Ezra as an avatar of Enoch. If such beliefs regarding Enoch were indeed projected onto the figure of 'Uzayr, that might explain the Qur'an's accusation against the Jews, although for the moment this remains entirely speculative. To the degree that this ancient Jewish mystic angelology may also have from the very beginning influenced Christian doctrines of the cosmic Christ, it is a path worth exploring.[23]

Whatever the case, Islamic commentary on the verse in question insists that this belief is not shared by all Jews. Some exegetes limited the scope of the accusation, holding that it was directed against a belief from the distant past and remarking that no similar blasphemy was to be found among the Jews of their time. Others maintained that this idea was never held by more than a small group of Jews. According to yet others, a single Jew exhibited this belief, a certain Finḥas. This commentary is above all to be found in medieval exegesis of the Qur'an, the writings of Tabari and Qurtubi, for example.

The Muslim sources have an equivocal relationship to 'Uzayr. On the one hand, he is seen as one of the prophets of the people of Israel, as is made clear for example in al-Tha'labi's (d. 1035) *Qiṣaṣ al-anbiya'* ("Stories of the Prophets"), and he is said to have played a central role in teaching the Bible to the Jewish people following their return from the Babylonian exile. According to the Muslim sources, when the Jews returned from exile in Babylonia, they had lost the Torah "and their hearts forgot it." 'Uzayr wept over and bemoaned this loss. According to one version of the story, while he was plunged in mourning, an angel appeared to him in the form of a man and asked what was afflicting him and why he cried. 'Uzayr told him that it was the loss of the Torah that saddened and grieved him. The angel asked him to fast, purify his clothing, and meet him at the same spot the next day. The next day, the angel arrived. He had him drink from a container held in his hand (according to another version, a heavenly light spread over him) and in this way the Torah once again dawned in his memory and he set about writing it down for the children of Israel. 'Uzayr could now teach the Torah to his people.[24]

One finds different versions of this story in many Muslim sources—for example, in Tabari's monumental work of history, which presents a positive portrait of 'Uzayr as having revived Moses' teaching. According to Tabari, it is perhaps this role played by 'Uzayr in rediscovering the lost Bible that explains his people's admiration for him, with some going so far as to see him as the son of God. These notions are well known in the rabbinical literature, which recounts that, when the exiled returned from Babylonia, 'Ezra reconstructed the text of the Torah on the basis of three old copies (*Jerusalem Talmud,* Ta'anit 4:2) and that it was he who decided that it would henceforth be written in "Assyrian" characters (today's square Hebrew) rather than in the paleo-Hebraic alphabet (*Babylonian Talmud, Sanhedrin* 21b–22a).

'Uzayr's relationship to the rediscovery of the Torah also provided the basis for constructing a negative image of him. Muslim authors, beginning with 'Ali b. Aḥmad Ibn Ḥazm the Andalousian (d. 1064), saw 'Ezra as the figure most responsible for deforming and falsifying the Bible. In a polemical work targeting his illustrious compatriot, the poet, Talmudist, and Vizir to the Emir of Grenada al-Samw'al Ibn al-Naghrila (known as Shemu'el ha-Nagid), Ibn Ḥazm writes:

They [=the Jews] admit also that 'Ezra, who wrote (the Torah) for them from his memory after it was lost, was only a scribe (*warraq*) and not a prophet. But a certain group among them says that he was the son of God, and that group has disappeared . . . [25]

On this basis, Ibn Ḥazm began to present 'Ezra as a figure of malice, a villain who deliberately falsified the Hebrew Scriptures. His opinion significantly contributed to casting a shadow over the figure of 'Uzayr/'Ezra and went a good way toward ensuring that the positive image of him offered by older sources was forgotten or rejected.

Another important medieval figure who participated in the effort to present 'Ezra as the Bible's greatest falsifier was the apostate Jew al-Samaw'al al-Maghribi (d. 1175) in his work *Ifḥam al-yahud* ("Reduction of the Jews to Silence"). While he did not endorse the received notion that the Qur'an's 'Uzayr and the biblical 'Ezra were one and the same, al-Maghribi insisted on 'Ezra's falsification, evident for example in the licentious nature of King David's genealogy. In the same spirit as modern biblical criticism, which tends to detect in these writings the hand of a writer belonging to circles opposed to the court of the kings of Judea, al-Maghribi claimed that biblical accounts concerning Lot's licentious relations with his daughters (Gen. 19:30–38), and above all those of Juda and Tamar (Gen. 38:12–30), were deliberately introduced into the Torah by 'Ezra, a priest from the Levi tribe, in order to damage the house of David (from the Juda tribe) and undermine the legitimacy of its claims on the monarchy. As evidence of this claim, al-Maghribi added that, "in the time of the second temple, the government belonged to the priests of the house of Aaron (=Harun) and not to the monarchs of the house of David."[26] He is here referring to the Hasmonean Dynasty, which reigned after the Maccabean revolt against the Seleucid kings (140 to 37 BCE).

In addition to the anti-Jewish polemic, al-Maghribi's arguments, which are also to be found in Ibn Ḥazm, reveal a major difference of sensibility between Muslim and Jewish authors. For Muslims, the fact that the Torah attributes less than glorious behavior to the prophets is a sign of their perversity and indicates that the Jews falsified the text. For Jewish authors, by contrast, the fact that these episodes figure in the text of the Bible is evidence that it has not been altered: if someone were to have ventured to "correct" the Torah, he doubtless would have cut out these unflattering passages. This is the argument with which the Talmudist Salomon ben Adret (1235–1310) countered Ibn Ḥazm.[27]

Falsifiers of the Torah

The Qur'an and post-Qur'anic Muslim sources are characterized by an ambivalent relationship to the Bible: on the one hand, Islam considers the Bible to be among the holy scriptures that God revealed to men before offering the Qur'an to the Arabs and, more broadly, to humanity in general. This is why the Qur'an and then Muslims turned to the Bible to prove the Qur'an's veracity—just as the Christians had done before them Many Bible verses are moreover interpreted as predicting the future coming of Muhammad and the triumph of Islam. One example among many others is the verse, well-known to Jewish and Christian exegetes, who saw it as heralding the coming of the Messiah: "For unto us a child is born, unto us a son is given; and the government shall be upon his shoulder . . ." (Isaiah 9:6). This literal interpretation did not go unremarked by Muslim scholars, who however saw it as an allusion to Muhammad's prophetic mission. They placed their emphasis on the words: "government shall be upon his shoulder." Various Arabic terms were used to translate the word "government" (*misra* in Hebrew, from the root *s-r-y*, "having authority"), and Muslim scholars understood the biblical verse as speaking of the "Seal of the Prophet" which, according to Muslim belief, literally appeared on Muhammad's shoulder. They thus insisted that the verse could in no way be taken as an allusion to Jesus, whose shoulder bore no such sign, but only to Muhammad, whose body was, it was said, marked by the Sacred Seal.

On the other hand, Islam had since it first emerged contested the integrity of the biblical text as we know it. The Qur'an accuses the Jews of tendentiously falsifying (*taḥrif*) the latter and modifying (*tabdil*) the order of its verses: "Some of those who are Jews change words from their places . . ." (Q. 4:46, among others); "Woe to those who write the Scripture with their own hands and then say, 'This is from God'!" (Q. 2:79). The aim of these falsifications and modifications—which, as we have seen, Muslim tradition mainly ascribes to 'Uzayr/'Ezra—was thus to eradicate from the Bible all testimony relating to the future coming of Muhammad: the description of the individual, of his qualities, of the victory of the religion that he was destined to bring to humanity, and so on.

Ambivalence towards the Bible is unquestionably present in the Qur'an, and it has determined Islam's relationship to the Bible throughout its history. This ambiguity is perhaps also one reason why the Qur'an does not quote the Bible word for word. One of its striking characteristics is the fact that, while it very frequently paraphrases biblical accounts, it almost never literally reproduces a verse from the Bible. The only quasi-literal quotation of a biblical verse is "We have written in the Psalms after the Reminder, 'The earth will be inherited by My righteous servants'" (Q. 21:105), but even here the verse from Psalms is slightly different: "The righteous shall inherit the land,

and dwell therein forever" (Psalms, 37:29).[28] This strongly suggests that the Qur'an is interested in what it grasps of the Bible's content rather than in the manner in which it is expressed. The fact that the Bible is seen as having been falsified, in other words, is sufficient reason not to quote it. One may use the parts that have not been falsified, but one must avoid doing so indiscriminately. This attitude is diametrically opposed to that of Christianity, which in principle accepts the Bible as it is but sometimes interprets it differently.

Killers of Prophets

One of the most common and most serious accusations against the Jews is that they murdered the prophets who were sent to them: "Humiliation and poverty were stamped upon them and they incurred anger from God. This was because they did not believe in God's signs and wrongfully slew the prophets . . ." (Q. 2:61). And again: "In times past We took Covenant with the Children of Israel and We sent messengers to them. Whenever a messenger came to them with what their souls did not desire, a number they denied and number they killed" (Q. 5:70).

The Bible does not attest to either of these accusations from the Qur'an, nor to any instance of the specific charges they inspired; namely, that the Jews killed some particular prophet or another. Abraham Geiger held that it is the crucifixion of Jesus that is at issue here (even though the Qur'an claims that Jesus did not truly die on the Cross). Another possibility is that they refer to the assassination of the Zachary or Zechariah who was John the Baptist's father.[29]

Other scholars, Josef Horovitz among them, have linked this verse to a passage from the New Testament, which it echoes: "O Jerusalem, Jerusalem, you that kill the prophets, and stone them which are sent unto you!" (Matthew 23:37; Luke 13:34; Romans 11:3; I Thessalonians 2:14–15).[30] It cannot be ruled out that these passages are themselves inspired by the words of the prophet Elijah, who would thus have been familiar to the first Muslims: "I have been very jealous for the Lord God of hosts; for the Children of Israel have forsaken your Covenant, thrown down your altars and slain your prophets with the sword" (I Kings 19:10); "Your own sword has devoured your prophets, like a destroying lion" (Jeremiah 2:30).

The Qur'an adopts an ambiguous position regarding Jewish guilt for the crucifixion of Jesus. On the one hand, it places a confession in their mouths—"We killed Christ, Jesus, the son of Mary, the messenger of God" (Q. 4:157)—that is consistent with the reputation imputed to them as "killers of prophets and messengers." On the other, it also holds that Jesus was not in fact crucified: "They did not kill him nor crucify him but it was made to seem to them (*shubbiha lahum*)" (ibid.). The attitude of the Qur'an towards the crucifixion has been the object of extensive research, and the dominant opinion is that it here adopts the view of the Docetists. Associated with the Gnostics, this heretical sect held that Jesus was not human but rather a divine manifestation whose body was only apparent; he could not die and his crucifixion was a mere illusion.[31]

In the words of Elijah, discussed above and known to both the New Testament and the Qur'an, the prophets' murder thus expresses the abandonment of the Covenant. In other words, in abandoning the Covenant, the people so abased themselves that they killed God's messengers. While it remains uncertain whether this accusation was known to the first Muslims, there can be no doubt that it is supported as much by the Qur'an it-self, which mentions it nine times (although the Jews are not always explicitly identified), as it is by exegesis inspired by the anti-Jewish polemic.

These were the principal negative characteristics ascribed to the Jews, but there were others as well. The charge of usury is among the most widespread (see, for example, Q. 4:161 and Q. 5:62). But what counts is not an enumeration of the grievances directed against them, but above all the fact that this overarchingly negative vision of the Jews supplied a basis for de-legitimating and belittling them. It was their own sins that condemned the Jews to poverty and an inferior status: "Humiliation and poverty were stamped upon them" (Q. 2.61). And, as we shall see in Chapter 5, it was their own inferiority that made the *jizya* necessary, as a marker of their low station. Moreover, the Qur'an points out that compared to the relatively small number of Qur'anic prescriptions, a great many biblical commandments (613 according to Jewish tradition) were inflicted as divine punishment on the Jews.[32]

All of these accusations leveled against the Jews must be set in the context of an anti-Jewish polemical tradition that predated Islam. Several of them, including the breaking of the Covenant with God and the murder of prophets, were present in Christian polemic, and the Samaritans had already spread the idea that the Jews had falsified Scripture. The Jews as usurers, meanwhile, is an ancient slur. The causal relationship established by the Qur'an between the Jews' purported characteristics and the fact that God spurned them—whence their loss of legitimacy—also originates in pre-Islamic religious traditions. The famous paradigm of "mind" versus "body" and "love" versus "Law" first developed by Paul, shows that early Christianity already interpreted the yoke of the commandments as a punishment imposed upon the Jews, and not a sign of election.

Similarly, the Jews' submission to Christian power expressed the will of God, who had turned away from them because they refused to believe in Jesus. In this, the Qur'an is the heir to ancient stereotypes.

"Transformed into Apes and Pigs"

The Qur'an's claim (Q. 7:163 and Q. 2:65–66) that Jews were transformed into or reincarnated (*musikhu*) as apes because they had transgressed the Shabbat has enjoyed a long life in the post-Qur'anic literature. Another verse speaks more generally of People of the Book (*ahl al-kitab*)—and thus includes the Christians—being "transformed into apes and pigs" (Q. 5:59–60). The classical Sunni tradition sees this metamorphosis as a one-off episode and speculates as to its real or figurative meaning and what it might say about the porosity between the animal and human kingdoms and the fate of these apes: are all present-day apes descended from these transformed men?[33]

In other Muslim writings, in particular among what are known as "heterodox" or "exaggerating" (*ghulat*) Shi'i sects, these episodes were interpreted in the context of the doctrine of the transmigration of the human soul. Depending on the gravity of one's sins, the human soul might transmigrate in various ways, including into animals, with the various degrees of this transformation described by the rhyming words *naskh, maskh, waskh*, and so on.[34]

These Qur'anic verses inspired the expression *awlad al-qirada wa-l-khanazir*, "descendants of apes and pigs," one of the most common insults directed against Jews and Christians (as a quick search online will attest). More specifically, the Jews became "children of apes" and the Christians "children of pigs."

Internally, Muslim tradition questions whether these epithets are to be taken literally and whether they apply to Jews and Christians of all eras. In a maximalist reading of these verses, if "the Jews were transformed into apes," must one conclude that the Jews of today are in reality apes whose human form is only apparent? This reading is soundly dismissed by many Muslim sages on the grounds that divine justice would not allow descendants to be punished for the misdeeds of their ancestors. The insult nevertheless endures.

The Ḥadith of Stones and Trees

This process of delegitimizing the Jews, which in Muhammad's lifetime reached its apogee with the Jews' expulsion from Medina and its surroundings, as well as the massacre of the men of the Qurayza tribe and the enslavement of their women, has continued throughout Islamic history. The Jews are regularly accused of fomenting plots against Muhammad and seeking to subvert Islam. In the same spirit as one observes in the Qur'an and *Sira*, or biography of the Prophet, the literature of Ḥadith—that is, the oral traditions that trace their origins to the Prophet—is replete with pejorative reflections on the Jews. Haggai Ben-Shammai's article, "Jew-Hatred in the Islamic Tradition and the Koranic Exegesis," summarizes the ways in which the Jews are depicted in the literature of Ḥadith.[35]

One of the best-known of the ḥadiths is entirely atypical in that it presents the conflict between Islam and Judaism as an eternal struggle that will extend across all historical time and culminate only in the eschatological era: "The Day of Judgement will not come about until Muslims fight the Jews. When the Jew will hide behind stones and trees, the stones and trees will say, "O Muslims, O servant of God ('Abdallah), there is a Jew behind me, come and kill him! Only the *gharqad* tree, would not do that because it is one of the trees of the Jews."[36]

The "Ass Carrying Books"

The parable of the ass carrying books, which makes a number of appearances in Jewish literature (Andalusian authors such as Baḥya ibn Paquda and Yehuda al-Ḥarizi already cite it), summarizes the Qur'an's complex attitude towards the Jews: "The likeness (*mathal*) of those who have been loaded the Torah and then have not carried it is as the likeness of an ass carrying books" (Q. 62:5). Let us note in passing that the parable is introduced by the term *mathal*, "example, parable," recurs nearly one hundred times in the Qur'an and has an exact counterpart in the Midrashic literature, *mashal*, where it is frequently invoked as a device.

The Jews were thus "loaded" with the Torah—that is, with an important and venerable inheritance that the Qur'an does not minimize. Yet, though they are its custodians, they neglect it, carrying it merely in the most pedestrian of senses, as would an ass that does not know what he has on his back. Had the Jews been capable of recognizing the value of the inheritance confided upon them, they would have rectified their behavior, thereby making good use of it rather than deforming, falsifying, and rejecting it. If they had respected the divine inheritance in their conduct, they would not have been abandoned by God and condemned to the degradation and poverty to which the Qur'an reduces them. This type of reproach is not foreign to the Bible, where the prophets routinely rebuke the people. Isaiah, for example, declares: "The revelation of all these events remains for you like the text of a sealed book. Offer it to an illiterate in asking him to read, he answers: 'I am not learned'" (Isaiah 29:12). It must nevertheless be noted that the comparison of the Jewish people to an ass loaded with books also constitutes a warning to Muslims. Many men behave like these Jews in what concerns the Revealed Word; Muslims are thus encouraged to draw a lesson from this so as not to go astray as had the Jews.

More generally, it is worth asking: to whom is the Qur'an addressed? The verses criticizing the faithlessness of the Jews always seem to play a twofold role. On the one hand, they serve to establish the Muslim community as the new "chosen people." But, at the same time, they put Muslims on notice: a Muslim who does not remain faithful to God's Word, is no better than these Jews.

III

Biblical Accounts and Their Transformations in the Qur'an

THE QUR'AN is replete with principles of faith, ideas, and accounts that would have been familiar to readers of the Bible and post-biblical literature. This is obvious even on a superficial reading of the Qur'an. Sometimes, however, recognizing these elements requires more effort as they have been significantly reworked to fit the Qur'anic narrative and its specific qualities and aims. Since the field of Islamic studies first emerged over two centuries ago, many scholars have studied these links. Of these, the most eminent include Abraham Geiger, Ignaz Goldziher, Helmut Speyer, David Sidersky, Josef Horovitz, Shlomo Dov Goitein, Hava Lazarus-Yafeh and Uri Rubin. Noteworthy also in recent years are the works of Sidney Griffith (*The Bible in Arabic: The Scriptures of the "People of the Book" in the Language of Islam*) and Gabriel S. Reynolds (*The Qur'an and the Bible: Text and Commentary* and *The Qur'an and Its Biblical Subtext*).

The Hebrew Vocabulary of the Qur'an

As we have seen, as a result of Muslims' contacts with different cultures, the Qur'an is marked by a religious terminology foreign to prehistoric Arabic. This is a phenomenon to which modern scholarship has devoted much attention, focusing either on particular terms and groups of words or by way of monographic studies of the subject, such as Arthur Jeffery's pioneering work, *The Foreign Vocabulary of the Qur'ān*. That book contains a very precise discussion of many important terms in the Qur'an that are of obvious biblical or post-biblical origin. These terms clearly would not have been used in the Qur'an had its writers not been in contact with Jewish sages. Among others, one may here cite such eschatological expressions as *yawm al-din*, "the day of [last] judgment," which might come from the Hebrew *yom ha-din*; *Jahannam*, or Gehenna, which comes from the word *gehinnom* or *gehinnam*; *jannat 'adn*, "the Garden of Eden", derived from *gan 'eden*; and *Yajuj wa-Majuj*, "Gog and Magog," two apocalyptic peoples known from biblical (Ezekiel 38–39) and Qur'anic eschatology. The Qur'an mentions them in connection with the exploits of Alexander, who is referred to in the text as "the two-horned man," *Dhu l-qarnayn* (Q. 18:82–98). One finds yet other examples: the word *ḥabr* (pl. *aḥbar*), referring to a Jewish sage or rabbi and derived from *ḥaber*, a Hebrew term referring to a "colleague," a member of rabbinic circles; *asbat*, "tribes" (sing. *sibt* but only occurring in its plural form in the Qur'an), which comes from the Hebrew *shebet* (pl. *shebatim*), referring to the twelve tribes of Israel that originated with the twelve sons of Jacob—the word still appears, moreover, in the expression *Ya'qub wa-l-asbat* ("Jacob and the tribes") and in the phrase *wa-qatta'nahumu thnata 'ashrata asbata* ("We divided them into twelve tribes") (Q. 7:160); *Sakina*, which very likely comes from the Hebrew word *shekhina*, a typically rabbinic expression referring to the "Divine Presence";[1] *'elyon*, a Hebrew adjective reminiscent of *'illiyyun*, meaning "supreme," "above" in references to the heavenly world; and *shaytan*, named after his biblical homologue *Satan*, the Devil. I will conclude this partial enumeration with the well-known words *ṣalat* ("prayer") and *zakat* (charity), which refer to two of the future five pillars of Islam. They likely derive from the words *ṣelota* and *zekhuta* in Aramaic/Syriac, a language used in this period by Eastern Jews and Christians alike.

The Qur'an and Genesis

In echoing the Bible, the Qur'an shows a pronounced taste for the Pentateuch in contrast to the other books of the Bible, which are notable for their complete absence. The heroes of Genesis are well represented, including Adam, Noah, Lot, Abraham and his sons, Jacob, and Joseph and his brothers. The prophet Moses, a central figure in the Qur'an, is the object of long narratives describing episodes of his life, in particular his confrontation with Pharaoh and his role as guide of the Hebrews from their departure from Egypt to their entry to the Holy Land. Other biblical figures, such as Saul (Talut), David and Goliath (Jalut), Solomon and Jonas, are mentioned sparingly, with brief allusions scattered here and there. Isaiah, Jeremy, and Ezekiel, the great prophets to whom the Bible devotes entire books, are passed over in total silence. Post-Qur'anic literature compensated for the conspicuous absence of such major biblical figures with the literary genre known as "stories of the prophets," *qiṣaṣ al-anbiya'*. These accounts include chapters on figures absent from the Qur'an, as well as figures mentioned only in passing, sometimes simply by name without further elaboration, like Elijah (Ilyas), Elisha (Alyasaʿ) and Job (Ayyub).

Another characteristic feature of these biblical—or, rather, semi-biblical—accounts is that the Qur'an often seems to rely more on post-biblical Jewish literature (Talmud and Midrash) than on the Hebrew Bible itself. Before examining these accounts, a few remarks are demanded regarding the nature of Qur'anic accounts. First and most striking is the observation that they are short, abbreviated, and elliptical. Indeed, it is very rare to find full, long and unbroken accounts. The same figure—Noah, Abraham, Lot, or Moses—may play a role in several passages of the Qur'an, but in each instance the account is fragmentary, so that in order to obtain a more complete picture of the particular figure, one must pull together repetitive or sometimes supplemental information from the various passages in which the individual appears. In the case of Noah, for example, one finds a detailed account in sura 11 (verse 25–48), sura 7 (verse 59–64), and sura 26 (verse 105–121), which cover, respectively, Noah's admonishment to his people, their refusal to listen to him, and the Deluge that overtakes them as punishment. In many other suras, moreover, Noah is briefly mentioned in relation to a few details of his life or that of his family—in Q. 66:10, for example, where his wife and Lot's wife are described as traitors; and in Q. 23:25, where it is said that Noah is accused by his kin of being possessed by djinns. None of these stories appears in the Bible. In Genesis, the dialogue between Noah and the people is also absent, for it is God who decides to send the Flood; the Qur'an for its part follows an outline that emphasizes the mission of the prophet (in this case, Noah), who denounces his people for their sins and, faced with their recalcitrance, announces the punishment.

One explanation for the elliptical nature of Qur'anic accounts is that the Qur'an does not seek to recount the entire story of any given biblical figure, but is rather content to mention it to a public already familiar with it. For this purpose allusion suffices. The *dh-k-r* root, equivalent to the Hebrew *z-kh-r* (recall, remember), thus recurs nearly three hundred times, like a leitmotiv: "Remember what was said . . ." It is even encountered in the introductions to these story cycles. In Q. 19:16, for example, the story of Marie/Myriam opens with *udhkur fi-l-kitab*, "Recall in the Book . . . !"; as does verse 41 of the story of Abraham; verse 51 of Moses; verse 54 of Ismael; and verse 56 of Idris, who is identified with Enoch. The mention of each prophet's name introduces the account of his story. The only exception is Joseph's story, for the sura concerning him is particularly long and detailed—something that is not unparalleled in the Torah, where the particularly long story of Joseph (fourteen of the fifty chapters contained in Genesis) almost reads like a novel.

Another characteristic trait of the Qur'an is that it often omits to mention an account's heroes by name. When it mentions Cain and Abel, for example, it simply refers to them as "the two sons of Adam." The case of Joseph and his brothers is similar: the Qur'an does not name any of Joseph's brothers but only his father Jacob, Joseph himself, and the figure known from Genesis only as Potiphar's wife, Potiphar being the Egyptian minister to whom Joseph had been sold as a slave and whom the Qur'an nicknames *imra'at al-'aziz* (the ruler's wife).

Another characteristic of these stories is that they direct moral commands and reprimands at the Qur'an's listeners and readers. This preoccupation doubtless explains why the narrative neglects facts relating to individuals: it is not the stories themselves that are important but the lesson that may be drawn from them. The prophets of the Qur'an, most or all of whom are also considered prophets in the Jewish tradition, are called "messengers" (*mubashshirun*) and "warners" (*mundhirun*). This is the essence of their mission and, as a result, that of Muhammad, who is their ultimate successor: to herald the word of God and warn against any and all offense against it. Thus Noah, who is seen as a prophet in the Qur'an (in contrast to the Bible, where he does not succeed in making himself heard and seems nearly mute), is a preacher who never ceases to speak, reprimand, and warn. In contrast with the Bible, the Qur'an says nothing about Noah's sons and does not mention their names; only one of them is his father's interlocutor and then is severely scolded by him.

Let us now examine a number of biblical accounts and the manner in which they are revisited in the Qur'an. It is clear that any choice can only offer an incomplete picture. The several examples I have chosen should, however, allow us to better evaluate the link between Qur'anic accounts and their counterparts in the Jewish sources.

Cain and Abel

As we have seen, the Qur'an does not mention their names but only vaguely evokes them as "the two sons of Adam" (Q. 5:27). They are referred to in the post-Qur'anic Muslim tradition, however, by a pair of rhyming names—Habil and Qabil— either in that order or inversely.

For the most part, the history of the two brothers as it is related in the Qur'an (5:27–32) is analogous to, but more concise than the biblical account (Genesis 4:1–16). According to the Qur'an's version, the two children brought a sacrifice to God, who only accepted the offering of one of them. Unlike the Bible, the Qur'an specifies neither the identity of the one who offered the acceptable sacrifice nor the nature of that sacrifice. From the Qur'anic sentence reading "God accepts only from those who are god-fearing" (Q. 5:27), one may deduce that it was Cain (as is affirmed by the Bible and Muslim tradition alike) who saw his offering refused because he was not motivated by fear of God. Moreover, as in the account of Genesis, the post-Qur'anic tradition—which, as usual, is more verbose—supplies more details regarding the causes of Cain's anger, which seem clearly to have been inspired by Jewish Midrashic traditions. Having devoted himself to agriculture, Cain chose as his offering the least beautiful of the fruits he had grown, while Abel, a shepherd, brought the most desirable animals of his herd. That God accepted Abel's sacrifice while refusing that of Cain angered the latter, prompting him to kill his brother.

The Qur'an and Jewish post-biblical sources mention two analogous additions to the biblical account. The first concerns the moral judgement brought to bear on the murder, and the second the issue of the victim's grave. The Qur'an denounces the gravity of the murder with the words:

> Because of that, We have prescribed for the Children of Israel that whoever kills a soul (*nafs*) other than in retaliation for [another] soul or for corruption in the land will be as if he had killed all the people; and whoever saves one will be as if he had saved the life of all the people. (Q. 5:32)

This equivalence between the murder of a single man and the destruction of humanity in its entirety already appears in ancient rabbinic exegesis of the reproaches that God addresses to Cain in Genesis 4:10. The Mishna comments:[2]

> Man was created single in order to show that to him who kills a single individual, it shall be reckoned that he has slain the whole race; but to him who preserves the life of a single individual it is counted that he has preserved the whole race.[3] (Mishnah, *Sanhedrin* 4:5).

The Qur'an further specifies the manner in which humanity's first murderer was brought to bury his victim:

> Then God sent a crow, which scratched into the earth to show him how he might hide the corpse of his brother. He said, "Woe on me. Am I unable to be like this crow and hide the corpse of my brother?" (Q. 5:31)

These details do not figure in the Bible but present certain analogies with the *Midrash Tanhuma* (regarding Genesis 10), which says:

> After Cain slew Abel, the body lay outstretched upon the earth, since Cain did not know how to dispose of it. Thereupon, the Holy One, blessed be He, selected two clean birds and caused one of them to kill the other. The surviving bird dug the earth with its talons and buried its victim. Cain learned from this what to do. He dug a grave and buried Abel.[4]

The general structure of this account, which appends elements that have their source in the rabbinic literature to a biblical core, is not unusual for the Qur'an.

Abraham

Of all the biblical prophets, Abraham occupies the most prominent place in the Qur'an. Sura 14 even bears his name, although only a few verses (35–40) speak about him. As is often the case with other figures, the information concerning him is dispersed throughout the text. Among the elements familiar from the Bible, one finds: the visit of the three angels who come to tell him of the birth of a son (Q. 11:69–76, with somewhat fewer details than Genesis); Abraham's quarrel with God regarding Sodom, although the town is not named and the "people of Lot" are simply mentioned in passing (*qawm Lut*, Q. 11:74–76 and Q. 29:32); the sacrifice of the birds (Q. 2:260), which refers to "the alliance of the pieces" (*berit bein ha-betarim*) (Genesis 15:1–21); and, above all, the sacrifice of Abraham's son (Q. 37:102–112).

This last episode assumed an important place in the Qur'an. Its telling is, however, very different from the account of Genesis. First of all, it is extremely adumbrated. Abraham does not receive a divine order to sacrifice his son. He says to the latter: "O my son, I have seen in my dreams that I shall sacrifice you. Look, what do you think?" (Q. 37:102). And his son responds: "O my father, do what you are commanded. You will find me, if God wills, to be one of the steadfast." The son accepts his fate without hesitation, not even asking, as Isaac had in the Bible: "Behold the fire and the wood: but where is the lamb for a burnt offering?" (Genesis 22:7). In the two accounts, God stops the hand of Abraham as he prepares to sacrifice his son, and a ram is sacrificed in his stead. The greatest difference between the two accounts resides in the identity of the son. Genesis specifies: "Take now your son, your only son Isaac, whom you love, and go into the land of Moriah; and offer him there for a burnt offering upon one of the mountains that I will tell you of" (Genesis 22:2). Several *midrashim* underscore the dramatic gradation in naming the victim:

And He said: Take, please, your son, etc. (22:2). Said God to him: "Take, I beg you—please—Your son." "Which son? I have two sons," he said. "Your only son," replied He. "This one is the only one of his mother, and this one is the only one of his mother." "The one you love"—"Is there a limit to the affections?" "Isaac," said He. And why did God not reveal it to him without delay? In order to make him [Isaac] even more beloved in his eyes and reward him for each and every word spoken. (*Genesis Rabbah 55:7*)

Contrary to a widely held belief, the Qur'an does not specify the son's identity, merely mentioning "the good news of a prudent son" (Q. 37:101). It is revealing in this connection that the "official" Saudi translation by Muhammad Hamidullah feels obliged to parenthetically specify "Ishmael"! It was the exegetes who subsequently attempted to respond to this question. The great Qur'an commentator Tabari reports a number of opinions, most of which (including his own) favor Isaac on the grounds that it was Isaac and not Ishmael who was the object of a divine announcement. Several other exegetes come down on the side of Ishmael, and this is now the most widespread opinion in Islam. It is far from being a matter of consensus, however, and has not always enjoyed majority support.

Alongside the biblical elements that seemingly converge in constructing the Qur'anic figure of Abraham, the Qur'an also extensively borrows from post-biblical Jewish literature. The most famous example of this is Abraham's debate with the idolaters of his time, whose statues he smashes (Q. 21:52–70; Q. 29:24; Q. 37:88–98), an episode that is absent from Genesis but amply chronicled in the midrash and very much present in Jewish culture, where it is seen as the inaugural gesture in Abraham's adoption of monotheism (see, for example, *Genesis Rabbah* 38:13). Abraham begins by claiming that it is vain to prostrate oneself before idols, and then proceeds to the belief in a single God and the rejection of other powers, whether of the stars or of idols:

> When the night came down on him, he (Abraham) saw a star. He said, "This is my Lord!"; but when it set he said, "I do not love things that set". When he saw the moon rising, he said, "This is my Lord!"; but when it set, he said, "If my Lord does not guide me, I shall be one of the people who go astray." When he saw the sun rising, he said, "O my Lord.

This is greater!"; but when it set, he said: "O my people, I am quit of what you associate with God." I have turned my face to Him who created the heaven and the earth, as a man of pure face, and I am not one of those who associate others with God." (Q. 6:76–79)

The discovery of the monotheistic truth via a meditation on cosmic phenomena is a widespread theme in pre-Qur'anic Jewish literature. The Qur'anic account reported here is strongly reminiscent of the pre-Christian *Book of Jubilees* (XII, 16–18), as well as of various midrashim, such as the passage of *Genesis Rabbah* (39:1) apparently comparing the world to an illuminated tower. From this, Abraham deduces that there must be someone who governs this tower, at which point God reveals himself, telling him, "It is I who govern this tower"—that is, the world.

According to various scholars, this vision of Abraham as the founder of monotheism owes much to the new direction taken by Muhammad after the *hijra*. In most of the Meccan suras, Abraham is presented as a prophet like the others, with no special status. By contrast, during the Medina period following Muhammad's break with the Jews, Abraham became a central figure and an example in the eyes of the Prophet. The Qur'an proclaims:

"Abraham was neither a Jew nor a Christian. He was a man of pure faith, one who surrendered (*hanif muslim*). He was not one of those who associate others with God" (Q. 3:67).

It goes without saying that, applied to Abraham, the term *muslim* does not mean that he belonged to Islam but rather that he was a true believer who had submitted to God.[5] This is also the meaning of *hanif*, a term of Syriac origin that is associated with *muslim* and in the Qur'an means "pure monotheism not affiliated with a particular religion."[6] The underlying goal here is to present

Abraham as the father of monotheism and thus deprive the Jews and Christians of their hegemony over Abraham and their claim upon him as the father of their respective religions. Thus, Islam does not conceive of itself solely as a new phase in the story of divine revelation, but also and perhaps above all as a return to an original monotheism that predated the religious divisions sadly exemplified by Jews and Christians. The Qur'anic verse *Inna al-din 'inda Allahi al-islam*, "Religion with God is submission [*islam*] (Q. 3:19), is read by 'Abd Allah b. Mas'ud, a famous companion of Muhammad, as *Inna al-din 'inda Allahi al-ḥanifiyya*, "Religion with God is the religion of the *ḥanifs*,"[7] which the subsequent portion of the verse clearly contrasts with the theological quarreling that divides Jews and Christians.

That Abraham is a unifying figure, the common father of Judaism, Christianity, and Islam is clearly indicated by the number of biblical and midrashic elements detectable in his Qur'anic biography. But he is also a specifically Islamic figure to the degree that Muhammad saw himself as an *Arab* prophet for whom Abraham was the archetype. Certain episodes from Abraham's life are thus supposed to have taken place on the Arabian Peninsula. As he himself proclaimed: "O Lord, I have made some of my seed dwell in a valley where there is no sown land close by Your Holy House . . ." (Q. 14:37). The "valley where there is no sown land" is that of Mecca, where the Ka'ba is located, which this verse refers to as a "Holy House." God points out its location to Abraham and tasks him with calling for pilgrimage: "Proclaim the pilgrimage to the people. Let they come to you on foot and on every lean camel, which will come from every deep ravine, to witness things of benefit for them and to mention the name of God on recognized days . . ." (Q. 22:27–28).

Abraham and his son Ismael are presented as advocating a heightened role for the Ka'ba, contributing to its Islamization, and promoting the pilgrimage to Mecca and its surroundings. The post-Qur'anic tradition further stresses this point: the route (sa'y) imposed on the pilgrims runs between the two hills of al-Ṣafa and al-Marwa and recalls that taken by Hagar in Genesis after Sarah drove her away as she sought water to quench her son Ishmael's thirst; and the well that, according to the Bible, she subsequently found with the assistance of an angel is said to be that of Zamzam, near the Ka'ba. It is thus clear that significant elements from the biblical story of Abraham were combined with other, typically Muslim tropes to create the image of an Arab prophet leading an active life on the Arabian Peninsula. In this way, Mecca—already a site of pagan worship—was transformed into a sanctuary of monotheism. This paved the way for Muhammad, whose mission was to bring the Arabs—indeed, all of humanity—to an *islam* already heralded by Abraham but now forgotten by the idolaters.

Joseph

The biblical account of Joseph also offers a good example of Muslim exegesis and the manner in which the Qur'an treats biblical and post-biblical Jewish sources. For the story of Joseph as it is recounted in Muslim texts very often echoes known *midrashim*, which among other things address various moments from the story of Genesis: Joseph being rebuked by his father for his dreams; his sale in Egypt; his error while imprisoned of trusting to the cupbearer rather than to God alone. A close reading of the full body of Muslim exegetical texts would doubtless discover many more vestiges of the midrash.

It is to be noted that the biblical and Qur'anic narratives have different beginnings. Genesis begins by mentioning Jacob's preference for his son Joseph, which understandably provokes his brother's jealousy, then continues with Joseph's dreams (the dream of the seven ears of grain and the dream of the sun, moon, and stars bowing down before him), the interpretation of which could only exacerbate his brothers' hatred. The second dream provokes a reprimand on the part of Jacob: "What is this dream that you have dreamed? Shall I and your mother and your brethren indeed come to bow down ourselves to you to the earth? And his brethren envied him; but his father observed the saying" (Genesis 37:10–11). The biblical account suggests an explanation for the brothers' hatred, which will later manifest itself when they confer with one another over whether they should kill him, throw him down a well, or sell him as a slave.

The Qur'anic account ignores the preference for Jacob and has Joseph recounting his dream about the sun, moon and stars bowing down at his feet only to his father. At this point Jacob warns his son, advising him not to tell his brothers of the dream for fear they will retaliate against him; he does not rule out the possibility that it is all a ruse of Satan. The brothers conclude that their father prefers Joseph and his brother (i.e., Benjamin, whose name is not mentioned however) without explicitly offering a reason: "Joseph and his brother are dearer to our father than we are, though there is a group of us. Our father is clearly in manifest error" (Q. 12:8).

The Qur'an also omits to mention that it was Jacob who sent Joseph to find his brothers, thereby leading him into the trap that resulted in his enslavement (Genesis 37:13–14). It was his brothers who insisted that Jacob send them Joseph: "O father, how is it that you do not trust us with Joseph? We really are his sincere well-wishers. Send him with us tomorrow and he can enjoy himself and play. We shall watch over him" (Q. 12:11–12). Thus, despite extensive similarities in their basic plots, the two accounts significantly diverge on certain points. The most obvious concerns the wife of Potiphar's attempt to seduce Joseph. Known in the Qur'an as *imra'at al-'aziz* (the ruler's wife), she became the heroine of their impossible love story in the classic Arabic novel *Yusuf and Zulaykha*.

The Qur'an states: "She verily desired him and he would have desired her if it had not been that he saw the proof of his Lord" (Q. 12:24). Whereas Joseph valiantly resists temptation in the biblical account—to give in would be to sin against God and against his master—in the Qur'an Joseph nearly gives way. Abraham Geiger and other scholars after him have drawn attention to the similarities between this passage of the Qur'an and various *midrashim* reported in the Talmud, including this one:

> "And she caught him by his garment, saying: Lie with me" (Genesis 39:12). At that moment his father's image came and appeared to him in the window, saying to him: "Joseph! Joseph! The names of your brothers are destined to be written on the stones of the Ephod and you are to be included among them. Do you desire your name to be erased from among them?" (*Babylonian Talmud, Sotah* 36b).[8]

The divergence between the biblical and Qur'anic accounts may thus be explained with reference to a post-biblical source, namely this Midrash. In both the Qur'an and the Midrash, it is the miraculous appearance of his father that, at the last minute, prevents Joseph from giving in to temptation. "The proof of his Lord" (*burhana rabbihi*) mentioned by the Qur'an does not seem to refer to a divine manifestation, but to the image of Jacob.

Several Qur'anic commentators mention Jacob's appearance before his son Joseph. One of them writes: "When Joseph saw before him the image of his father biting his fingers, he jumped with fright and water exited (a euphemism for an emission of sperm) his big toe."[9] This enigmatic description (that is, sperm issuing from the toe) itself resonates with a little-known *midrash* (though the kabalistic literature makes a great deal of it). In explaining the expression that Jacob used in blessing his son Joseph—"and the arms of his hands were made strong (*wayafozzu zero'ei yadaw*)" (Genesis 49:24)—the Talmud recounts that, to master his desire, Joseph "drove his hands into the ground and an emission of sperm (*zera'*) exited his fingernails and his fingers." This rabbinic reading was provoked by the pleonasm, "the arms of his hands" (*zero'ei yadaw*), which was then read as *zera' yadaw* ("the seed [i.e., the sperm emitted by] his hands"). In entering the Muslim exegetical tradition, the midrash lost what had justified it in the biblical verse and became an element of "legend."

Another anecdote deserves our attention. According to the Qur'anic account, after having confessed her sin, Potiphar's wife justified herself before the townswomen, putting them to the test in their turn so that they would understand the temptation to which she had been subjected:

> Some women in the city said: "The ruler's wife is trying to seduce her young man. He has smitten her heart with love. We think her clearly in the wrong!" When she heard their sly talk, she invited them and prepared for them a couch and gave to each of them a knife. Then she said to Joseph, "Go into their presence!" When they saw him, they admired him, and they cut their hands and said, "God is wonderful. This is not a mortal. This is nothing but a gracious angel." (Q. 12:30–31)

While no mention of this episode is to be found in the Bible, it does feature in the *Midrash Tanḥuma* and other midrashic sources:

> Potiphar's wife assembled a number of Egyptian women so that they might see how very handsome Joseph was. But before she summoned Joseph she gave each of them an ethrog

and a knife. When they saw Joseph's handsome countenance, they cut their hands. She said to them: "If this can happen to you, who see him only once, how much more so does it happen to me, who must look at him constantly." (*Midrash Tanḥuma*, parashat Wa-Yeshev 5)

In his article, "Joseph among the Ishmaelites: Q 12 in Light of Syriac Sources",[10] Joseph Witztum remarks that, in addition to the Jewish sources, those seeking to explain the Qur'an must also take into account some Christian sources, particularly the Syriac Church Fathers. This particular article examines aspects of the story of Joseph by comparing them to mostly fourth and fifth-century Syriac homilies, one written in prose and the others in rhymed poetry. These are, respectively, the homilies of Ephrem (d. 373) and those of Balai (active in the early fifth century) and Jacob of Serugh (d. 503). Alongside the comparisons that may be made between the Qur'anic account of Joseph and his brothers and post-biblical Jewish sources, Witztum here convincingly compares the Qur'an also with these Syriac sources. Since the latter differ from the biblical account in specific respects—the same omissions, the same elaborations and modifications—but none in a way that coincides with the Jewish sources, they suggest greater proximity.

The beginning of the account mentioned above offers an example of omission: neither the Qur'anic account nor the Syriac sources begin by explaining Jacob's marked preference for Joseph or the hatred that their behavior arouses among Joseph's brothers. Instead, any reproach that might be directed at Joseph is erased, and the story begins with an alternate version of Joseph's dreams. In the Bible, the hero recounts his first dream to his brothers and then recounts his second dream to his father, who rebukes him. In the Syriac sources and the Qur'an, by contrast, Joseph primarily wants to understand what these dreams—which he has reported only to his father—mean. Jacob forbids him from recounting them to his brothers, proof that he believes in them.

As for Potiphar's wife's attempt at seduction, according to Genesis, she slandered Joseph, had him thrown in prison, and then disappears from the story. As we have seen above, however, the Qur'an (Q. 12:50–54), like the Syriac sources, depicts her as confessing her sin and repenting. Despite these parallels, there are also a few differences. The Syriac sources emphasize Joseph's forgiveness and generosity, whereas the Qur'an underscores Joseph's innocence while at the same time depicting the repentance of Potiphar's wife.

Witztum also notes the typology embedded in this account. Following in the footsteps of other scholars, he underscores the two aims that guide the Qur'anic Joseph story: on the one hand, it seeks to encourage Muhammad in his struggle against his rivals, who are thereby warned of the fate awaiting non-believers; on the other, it seeks to present the Prophet as heir to the biblical tradition. In the Syriac literature, the interpretation of the story of Joseph also took a typological turn: just as in Qur'anic exegesis, where the enemies are not Jews but rather the people of Mecca, Joseph plays the role of Jesus and his brothers (the wolves of the story) that of the Jews.

David

Although it contains few details about him, David is nonetheless an important figure in the Qur'an. It presents him as a prophet and king, but makes little mention of the stories recorded in the books of Samuel, Chronicles, and Psalms. There are only brief allusions to his internal struggles and battles against the enemies of Israel, in particular against the Philistines (Q. 2:248–251). The only battle that is mentioned is the one that pitted him against Goliath (Jalut). Of his many sons and the rivalries that set them against one another or against him, only the name of Solomon (Sulayman) is mentioned. The Qur'an reports that, after his battle with Goliath, "God gave him sovereignty and wisdom and taught him some of what He wills" (Q. 2:251). In this verse, wisdom takes its bearings from the gift of prophesy. According to many commentators of the Qur'an, God's bestowal of knowledge upon David and his son Solomon (Q. 27:15) meant that they received the power to understand the language of birds and animals, as is reported also in certain *midrashim*. God is said to have made David his lieutenant (*khalifa*) on earth (Q. 38:26), a status he had formerly only granted to Adam (Q. 2:30). It is claimed that he also conferred upon him the privilege of distinguishing between truth and lie. This is why David is represented as sitting in judgement alongside his son Solomon:

> And David and Solomon, when they gave judgment concerning the tilled land, when the people's sheep had browsed in it by night and We bore witness to their judgement. We made Solomon understand it; and to each [of them] We gave judgement and knowledge. (Q. 21:78–79)

Moreover, David occupies a place apart alongside Moses, Jesus, and Muhammad in that he received from God a revealed Book, *al-Zabur*, which is generally identified with the Psalms (Q. 4:163 and Q. 17:55).

Sura 38 contains the Qur'an's longest reference to David. It opens with the Arabs mocking Muhammad: they reproach him for seeking to fabricate a single divinity out of the many others to whom they are attached. And, in reaction to Muhammad's preaching announcing the coming of the Last Judgement, they cry: "Our Lord, Hasten for us our share before the day of Reckoning" (Q. 38:16). Immediately thereafter, Muhammad reminds them that "Our servant David, the man of right [. . .] He was a penitent" (Q. 38:17) and alludes to the episode of David's relationship with Bathsheba by drawing upon the image of the rich shepherd who wants to carry off the poor shepherd's only sheep.

The prophet Nathan, who is the author of this parable in the Bible and who reprimands David for the grave sin he has committed, is not mentioned in the Qur'an, and the parable is transformed into a conversation between two men who stand trial before David:

> Have you heard the story of the dispute when they walled the sanctuary? When they went in to see David and he took fright of them? They said, "Do not be afraid! We are two disputants, one of whom has wronged the other. So judge between us with truth and do not transgress; and guide us to the level path. This is my brother. He has ninety-nine ewes, and I have one ewe. He said: 'Entrust it to me!' and he overcame me in talking to me"; [David] said: "He has wronged you in asking you to add your ewe to his. Many partners wrong each other, except those who believe and do good works, and they are few." David guessed that We have tested him, and he sought forgiveness from his Lord and he fell in prostration and repented. So We forgive him that. He had nearness to Us and a fair resort. "O David! We have made you a viceroy in the land. Judge between the people in truth. Do not follow caprice lest it lead you away from the way of God . . ." (Q. 38:21–26)

Anyone unfamiliar with the story of David's sin in taking the spouse of Uriah the Hittite (II Samuel 11:1–27) or with the parable of the poor man's sheep that is applied to David on account of that sin (12:1–25) could understand nothing of this passage from the Qur'an. The only allusion to these episodes is David's request for forgiveness (and the reader is not told what he is guilty of) and the exhortation to not act upon his passion (which the reader might interpret as moral advice of a general kind rather than a response to a particular offence). There is no doubt that, in this case also, the key to the passage is to be found in the biblical account.

Yet another important difference with the biblical account must be noted. Whereas the Bible does not seek to pass over embarrassing details of its heroes' lives in silence, but instead presents both their weaknesses and their good qualities, the Qur'an avoids as much as possible any hint of possible faults. Indeed, this tendency, subsequently broadened, became an established doctrine known as 'iṣmat al-anbiya' ("immunity of prophets [from sin and error]"), according to which the prophets were subject to neither sin nor error. Muslim theologians and Qur'an commentators made considerable efforts to purify the prophets and other holy figures (particularly the Imams in Shi'i Islam) of anything that might tarnish their image in the Qur'an or in the external traditions that made their way into Muslim literature.[11]

Projecting a spotless image of the heroes of holy history while blackening the image of its antagonists was already very much a pattern in post-biblical Jewish literature. Attempts to cleanse David of the sin of adultery with Bathsheba are also encountered in the rabbinic literature, patently contradicting the letter of the biblical text, which supplies abundant details of that incident and even records that, following his reprimand by the prophet Nathan, David recognized the error of his ways (II Samuel 12:13

and Psalms 51). In a famous formula, the Talmud ties itself into exegetical knots to prove David innocent: "Anyone who says that David sinned [with Bathsheba] is nothing other than mistaken."[12] Because, the Talmud explains, at a legal (if not moral) level, David was guilty of no transgression, especially as Uriah had divorced Bathsheba before leaving for war so that she might remarry should he die in combat without a witness. Therefore, David did not sleep with a married woman; at most, he is reproached for having been too pressed to marry the woman for whom he had been destined "since the six days of the Creation." This effort to clear David's name, the first stirrings of which are perceptible in the Qur'an, is even more extensively embroidered in post-Qur'anic literature. Pierre Lory summarizes the Muslim attitude as regards David's sin as follows:

> David's very serious sin no longer results from an uncontrolled carnal tendency: it is a trial induced by God, the aim of which is the prophet's moral and spiritual progress. Despite the gravity of his action, David comes away from it with his stature enhanced. Moreover, and in a more secondary way, the possibility that one of the most spiritual of prophets might at the same time possess a large harem allowed the Muslims to refute the criticism of some Medina Jews concerning the number of Muhammad's wives.[13]

A. H. Johns underscores the link between the figures of David and Muhammad. In his view, it is no accident that David is mentioned; the aim of doing so is to establish an analogy between them and present David as a source of inspiration for Muhammad. Both are prophets subjected to the mockery of their people. But just as David succeeded in all of his undertakings, internal and external alike, so Muhammad would succeed in his.[14]

Saul/Talut

Saul, the first king of Israel, is mentioned in the Qur'an (Q. 2:247 and 249) under the name Talut, after the pattern of Jalut, the Arabic name of Goliath, who appears immediately thereafter. (One finds other names formed along the same lines, such as the two pairs Ya'juj wa-Ma'juj [Gog and Magog] and the angels Harut and Marut (Q. 2:112), who according to the Qur'an's rendition of Genesis 6:4 and its midrashic expansions were deprived of their status after compromising themselves with the daughters of humans.) All commentators share the view that the name Talut comes from the Arabic root *t-w-l*, which means "to be tall." It seems that the Arabic name retains the memory of Saul's great height, which the Bible describes as follows: "There was not among the children of Israel a goodlier person than he; from his shoulders and upwards he was higher than any of the people" (I Samuel 9:2). Only the post-Qur'anic tradition—for example, al-Tha'labi's work, *Qiṣaṣ al-anbiya'* (Stories of the Prophets), retains his Hebrew name, which is joined to that of his father as it appears in the Bible: Sha'ul b. Qish.[15]

Like the stories of other biblical figures in the Qur'an, Saul's story is recounted with great concision. In a passage consisting of just four verses (Q. 2:246–250), one finds several elements extensively covered in the Bible: the people of Israel's request that their prophet (whose name is not specified but whom the exegetical tradition, in keeping with the Bible, generally identifies as Samuel) give them a king; Saul's selection of a group of men from his people to go fight their enemies; and, finally, the choice of David to confront Goliath and David's victory over the latter.[16]

The people of Israel's request that their prophet supply them a king to lead them in their fight against the enemy perfectly coincides with the biblical account found in I Samuel 8:4–22. Yet the Qur'anic account differs from the latter in what regards the people's reaction when the king was chosen. The Bible merely alludes to the reaction of a minority: "But the children of Belial said, How shall this man save us? And they despised him, and brought him no presents" (I Samuel, 10:27). The Qur'an, by contrast, reports that Saul/Talut's nomination aroused the opposition of all the people: "How can he have sovereignty over us when we have a better right to it than him since he has not given any abundance and possessions?" (Q. 2:246). Qur'an commentators, Tabari among them, explain that the people of Israel based their opposition on the fact that Talut belonged to the not particularly prestigious tribe of Benjamin, which distinguished itself neither by prophesy (like the Levi tribe) nor by royalty (like that of Juda).[17]

It is likely that the tradition according to which Saul was opposed on account of his ancestry echoes words that the Bible has Saul himself speak. When Samuel announces his election as king of Israel by telling him, "And on whom is all the desire of Israel? Is it not on you and on all your father's house?" (I Samuel, 9:20), Saul reacts with astonishment and humility: "Am I not a Benjamite, of the smallest of the tribes of Israel? And my family the least of all the families of the tribe of Benjamin? Wherefore then speak you to me?" (9:21).

According to the Qur'an, when faced with the people of Israel's opposition, their prophet firmly retorted that "God has chosen him over you and has given him a generous increase of knowledge and of strength" (Q. 2:247). Moreover, the verse continues, "God gives his sovereignty to those whom He wishes"—that is, to Saul/Talut. In order to persuade the sons of Israel to submit to the kingship of Saul, God places the sign of his kingdom before their eyes: "The sign of his sovereignty is that the ark, in which there is an assurance from your Lord, will come to you and a remnant of that which the family of Moses and Aaron left behind" (Q. 2:248). As Régis Blachère remarked in regards to this passage, "[t]here is hardly need to underscore the parallel made here between the advice of the Israelites who rejected the kingship of Saul and the advice of the Meccans and Medina Jews who refused to recognize Muhammad."[18]

Another episode to which the Qur'an alludes concerns the selection of warriors meant to fight the enemies of Israel. The Qur'anic text does not name these enemies but later tradition specifies—once again in keeping with the biblical text—that they were Canaanites or Amalekites. Talut chose his combatants by subjecting each to the test of drinking water from a river: "God will test you by means of a river," Saul (Talut) said to his men. "'Those who will drink from it are not of [my party] but those who do not taste it—and that does not exclude those who scoop up a little in the hand—are of [my party]'. But they drank from it, except for a few of them" (Q. 2:249). Those who drank the water—that is, a majority of the people—immediately proved that they were incapable of fighting Goliath, but the minority who did not—according to tradition, roughly 310 men—were ready to wage battle against a much larger army and even defeat it. It is to be noted that this episode is reported in the Bible not of Saul, but of Gideon, who subjected his warriors to a similar test before setting off to fight the Midianites (Judges 7:4–7).

The people's victory under David's leadership over enemies led by Goliath is very briefly recounted. What's more, the epic battle described in the Bible (I Samuel 17–18) is passed over in total silence. In a few words, the Qur'an reports that "David killed Goliath and God gave David sovereignty and wisdom and taught him some of what He wills" (Q. 2:251). This lacuna, strongly felt by Muslim tradition, was largely filled in post-

Qur'anic literature. Muslim exegetical and historical writings report much of what the Bible and the Midrash tell concerning the relations of Saul and David—for example, in Tabari's monumental *Universal History*. These works abound in colorful accounts of Saul's jealousy vis-à-vis David following the latter's stunning victory over Goliath, as well as of Saul's pursuit of David. Even nuances absent from the Midrash occur. Most remarkable of all is the tradition according to which Saul acknowledged the sinfulness of his feelings of jealousy towards David and, to win forgiveness for it, was ready to sacrifice his life and those of his children to God in the fight against his people's enemies.

The Red Heifer (*al-baqara*)

Al-Baqara, "The Cow," is the title of the Qur'an's second sura, thus called because it mentions the commandment of the red heifer (Q. 2:67–73). It is worth recalling here this very peculiar arrangement, which in Jewish tradition symbolizes the unfathomability of divine prescription. The book of Numbers (Ch. 19) describes the ritual as necessary to cleanse oneself of the impurity contracted upon contact with a cadaver. The priests must take an entirely red heifer that has never been under the yoke, fully burn it and mix its cinders in running water. The "lustral water" thus obtained is to be sprinkled on the impure individual on the third and seventh days following contact with a cadaver.

The description given by the Qur'an of this commandment, which takes the form of a dialogue between Moses and the people of Israel, in many respects resembles that of the Bible. Moses transmits the divine commandment to the people of Israel: "God commands you to sacrifice a heifer" (Q. 2:67). The Israelites are astonished and suppose that Moses is mocking them. When he repeats his words and assures them of his sincerity, they ask him to seek information from God regarding the nature of this heifer. Moses offers clarification: "She is to be a heifer that is neither old nor immature, but one whose age is between these" (Q. 2:68). But this response still did not satisfy them: "They said, 'Call to your Lord and let Him make clear to us what [kind] she is to be. All cattle are much the same to us . . .'" (Q. 2:70). Moses then provides additional information: "He says, 'She is to be a heifer not broken in to turn over the ground nor to water the tilled land, [but] kept sound, with no blemish on her'" (Q. 2:71). While the Qur'anic description is much more concise than that found in the Bible, the two are similar in what concerns the characteristics of the cow herself.

By contrast, when the Qur'an explains the meaning of the commandment, it completely departs from the biblical prescription, stating that: "And [recall] when you killed a soul and disagreed concerning it and God brought out what you were concealing, We said, 'Strike him with a part of it.' Thus God brings the dead to life" (Q. 2:73). Here, the Qur'an revisits another biblical commandment, one that also features a heifer never put to the yoke, which in this case is referred to as "the heifer whose neck has been broken" ("'egla 'arufa" in Hebrew). Here is the biblical text:

If one be found slain in the land which the Lord your God gives you to possess it, lying in the field, and it be not known who has slain it. Then your elders and your judges shall come forth and they shall measure unto the cities which are round about him that is slain. And it shall be that the city which is next unto the slain man, even the elders of that city shall take a heifer, which has not been wrought with and which has not drawn in yoke. And the elders of that city shall bring down the heifer unto a rough valley, which is neither eared nor sown, and shall strike off the heifer's neck there in the valley ... And all the elders of that city, that are next unto the slain man shall wash their hands over the heifer that is beheaded in the valley and they shall answer and say, 'Our hands have not shed this blood, neither have our eyes seen it.'" (Deuteronomy 21:1–7)

As scholars have shown, including Abraham Katsh in his book *Judaism in Islam*, the Qur'an here conflates two distinct biblical themes: the episode of the red heifer and that of the heifer whose neck had been broken. Katsh also takes note of the fact that ancient rabbinic literature linked these two biblical prescriptions, discussing them jointly (for example, in the *Sifrei*— that is, the Halakhic midrash regarding the books of Numbers and Deuteronomy). From this, Katsh concludes that "it is likely that the frequent Talmudic comparisons between the red heifer and the heifer whose neck had been broken led Muhammad to conflate the two episodes."[19]

The Midrash and the *isra'iliyyat*

The Qur'anic accounts of biblical figures have many parallels not only in the Bible, but also in Jewish post-biblical literature. In other words, many themes of rabbinic exegesis are taken up in the biblical episodes reported in the Qur'an as if they were an integral part of the Bible. At the same time, many biblical details are completely passed over. A few generations after the Qur'an was completed, Muslim men of letters, having considerably improved their knowledge of the Bible and rabbinic sources, produced an extremely rich exegetical literature. Thus, the collections of Ḥadith and, in particular, the literary genre mentioned above—that of "the stories of the prophets"—abound in biblical and post-biblical details.

All of the midrashim to which the post-Qur'anic Muslim tradition appeals are grouped together under the name *isra'iliyyat* (accounts and fables originating from or attributed to the children of Israel). Ignác Goldziher, a pioneering scholar of the *isra'iliyyat*, divided them into three categories: (a) remarks and accounts complementing the information given by the Qur'an on biblical themes, a type of *isra'iliyyat* found throughout Muslim literature; (b) texts known as *'ahd bani isra'il* (the era of the children of Israel), which despite this name contain no allusions whatsoever to Hebraic figures; and (c)folkloric and miraculous accounts of only partly Jewish origin.

The *isra'iliyyat* of the first category, which are particularly substantial, serve to fill in the many lacunae that characterize the Qur'anic accounts. Yet the Muslim sources that make use of them do not specify their origins. Like the biblical episodes, paraphrased but not literally translated by the Qur'an, the *isra'iliyyat* were carefully rewritten and adapted. Tracing their origin is thus difficult. They are cited after a vague introduction of the type, "I found in the Torah," "it is written in the Torah," or "it is written in the books" (*maktub fi-l-kutub*), expressions that do not necessarily refer to the Pentateuch or even to the Bible, but may instead designate material drawn from post-biblical literature. Pinning down these *isra'iliyyat* therefore requires an exhaustive knowledge of Jewish and Christian literatures.

The essential links in this transmission of sources were clearly Jewish converts to Islam and Muslim men of letters who were in contact with their Jewish and Christian counterparts. According to Muslim historical texts, these traditions were put into writing over a period of roughly one hundred years, beginning in the late seventh century. The book known as *Kitab al-isra'iliyyat* is attributed to Wahb b. Munabbih, a famous Muslim scholar of Jewish origin, and was apparently the first instance of the genre.[20]

A few examples among the copious teaching of Midrashim appear in both Sunni and Shi'i Ḥadith collections. This is the case of the story of Joseph. Muslim traditions discuss several episodes from this story, such as the brothers' disagreement regarding Joseph's fate, his sale as a slave to the Egyptians, his punishment for disrespecting his father, and the error of entrusting himself to Pharaoh's minister rather than to God while in prison.[21] In many traditions, moreover, the description of the Divine Throne and the four angels surrounding it recalls the "Divine Chariot" evoked in the prophesy of Ezekiel.[22]

The massive use of this Midrashic information in Muslim religious literature has yet to receive the attention it merits and, despite the work of the eminent Islamic scholars mentioned above, countless texts remain to be studied.

IV

Qur'anic Law and Jewish Law

THROUGHOUT THEIR HISTORIES, there has been considerable overlap between the religious laws of Judaism and those of Islam. We will in this chapter focus mainly on the Qur'anic strata of Islam, and especially on the sections dealing with the law, which are believed to belong to the period after the *hijra* of 622. While the suras of the Meccan period have apocalyptic and eschatological orientation, those of Medina are more juridical. In Mecca, Muhammad was persuaded that the end of the world was near, and this mindset is reflected in the Meccan suras, at least the oldest of them, which evoke the resurrection of the dead and the Last Judgment. In these same sura, questions of law are almost completely absent and only two religious obligations are mentioned: prayer (*ṣalat*) and almsgiving (*zakat*), with nothing said about how they were to be observed.

By the end of this Meccan period, and particularly after the *hijra*, the notion that the end of time was at hand had already begun to fade. Apocalyptic visions yielded primacy to the fight against the Arabs of Mecca, to spreading Islam, and to dialogue with the Jews of Medina. It was at first hoped that the latter might be converted to the new religion, but as we shall see, they subsequently became objects of growing hostility. It was at this point that the juridical dimension came to the fore. The very detailed legislation of this period concerns the army and war, the distribution of spoils, prayer, fasting, pilgrimage, the purity and impurity of women after menstruation or childbirth, dietary rules, permitted or forbidden animals, and lending at interest, among other topics.

Scholars unanimously attribute the prominence given legal questions in the Medina Qur'an to the influence of the local Jewish community. For a great number of specialists, the similarity between Muslim and Jewish jurisprudence is unsettling, for it appears that many of the Qur'anic laws presuppose a constant dialogue with biblical and post-biblical *halakha* (Jewish law). But clearly, the followers of the two religions lived in close proximity to one another. Moreover, some of the Qur'anic juridical themes evolved in pace with Islam's changing attitude towards Judaism.

In the second half of the nineteenth century, comparative research into the juridical ties between Islam and Judaism began to assume an important place in Islamic studies. In his book *Muhammad and the Jews of Medina*, originally published in Dutch in 1908, Arent Jan Wensinck extensively considers the manner in which Jewish sources influenced the development of Muslim worship. He shows that, in even their smallest details, the basic commandments of Islam, like prayer and fasting, resemble analogous injunctions in Judaism, going so far as to describe the latter as having inspired the former. Fixed hours of prayer and requirements for ritual purification and a particular geographic orientation prior to prayer are fundamental normative and liturgical principles common to both religions. It seems unlikely that these regulations would have taken their final form in Islam had there been no knowledge of Judaism, but the question has nevertheless been a source of debate within Islamic studies since the earliest days of the discipline. That it continues to roil contemporary research is demonstrated by contributions on this theme such as Robert Brunschvig's studies, "Herméneutique normative dans le judaïsme et dans l'islam"[1] and "Vœu ou serment?: Droit comparé du judaïsme et de l'islam."[2] A few years ago, Haggai Mazuz's book *The Religious and Spiritual Life of the Jews of Medina* (Leiden, 2014), built upon older studies such as those of Wensinck, Brunschvig, and many others after them. In this book, Mazuz examines a series of religious aspects of Medinan Judaism that left their mark on emergent Islam. He devotes his second chapter to *halakha* and customs, closely examining such subjects as Shabbat, fasting, prayer, marriage, adultery and its punishment, the laws of conjugal purity, the laws of war. His methodology brings to light the degree to which Medinan Judaism resembles or, to the contrary, diverges from rabbinic Judaism.[3]

We have seen that the Qur'an echoes biblical accounts without citing the Torah word for word. The links that connect legal rules in the Qur'an, the Bible, and postbiblical writings are likewise not the result of textual borrowing. In other words, it is not a matter of direct citations but rather of general thematic resemblance. At times, however, one is not far from word-for-word citation, as in the case of the *lex talionis*, or "law of an eye for an eye." The Qur'an expresses it as follows:

> We prescribed for them in it (i.e., in the Torah): a soul for a soul; an eye for an eye; a nose for a nose; an ear for an ear; a tooth for a tooth; and wounds [carry] retaliation. (Q. 5:45)

This is very close to the formulation in Exodus:

> And if any mischief follows then you shall give life for life, eye for eye, tooth for tooth, hand for hand, foot for foot,

burning for burning, wound for wound, stripe for stripe. (Exodus 21:23–25)[4]

Such resemblances cannot be a matters of accident. What's more, the manner in which the Talmud interprets these verses— not according to their apparent meaning, but in terms of a financial compensation proportional to the damage caused (since the impairment caused by a wound to the leg is not the same for an athlete as it is for a writer)—also seems to be echoed in the Qur'an:

O you who believe, retaliation is prescribed for you concerning the slain: the free man for the free man; the slave for the slave; the female for the female. For the [killer] who receives some forgiveness from the brother of [the slain], prosecution according to what is recognized as proper and payment to [the brother] in kindness. That is an alleviation and mercy from your Lord. Those who transgress after this will have a painful torment. (Q. 2:178)

Since the first centuries of Islam, Qur'an commentators and Muslim jurists have debated the issue of how to reconcile these two Qur'anic verses: do they really say the same thing (and what precisely?), or is the contradiction insurmountable, in which case one of the two verses abrogates the other. But which is to be abrogated (*mansukh*) and which is doing the abrogating (*nasikh*)? The various legal schools of Islam disagree on this question, as on many others. What matters for us is that the Qur'an adopts the two positions familiar from Jewish sources: a strictly literal interpretation of the law of an eye for an eye and a milder interpretation ("a mercy accorded by your Lord").

This short book is not the place to discuss all parallels between Jewish and Muslim law. I shall instead look at four essential topics: prayer (*ṣalat*) and, more specifically, the question of the direction to be adopted by the Muslim believer in prayer (*qibla*); fasting (*ṣawm*); dietary laws; and the fixing of the calendar. For our purposes, these four themes are revealing, not just of Judaism's proximity to Islam, but above all of the manner in which Islam was developed at once with reference to, and against Judaism.

The Laws of Prayer and *qibla*

In pre-Islamic Arab communities there were no daily prayers that might have served as a model for Muslim prayer. According to early Muslim sources, however, ritual formulae were recited by pagan Arabs when on pilgrimage to the various sanctuaries scattered across the Arabian Peninsula. These were above all expressions affirming faith and loyal service to the gods, seeking their counsel, and invoking their blessing before various undertakings. Given that we have no source attesting to pre-Islamic prayer, it is worth noting that before the advent of Islam, there was no Arabic word for "prayer"; the Qur'anic term *ṣalat* is not of Arab origin but was borrowed from the Aramaic *ṣelota*, a term used by both Jews and Christians in the Middle East. This word does not appear in pre-Islamic poetry, and one may suppose that it entered the Arabic language only after the emergence of Islam. It was probably adopted from Jewish and Christian speakers of Aramaic or Syriac with whom the Arabs were in contact.

Neither the structure of Muslim prayer nor its content resembles those of Jewish prayer. The former is distinguished for its simplicity and great brevity, the latter for its lengthy texts and long duration. There nevertheless exist significant commonalities in the ways in which prayer is conducted.

In both religions, a central role is played by intention (*niyya* in Arabic) and the issue of orientation (*qibla*) assumes an important place. According to Muslim tradition, prior to the establishment of the formula used in the muezzin's call to prayer (the *adhan*), it was customary to sound the Jews' *shofar* (*buq al-yahud*), or ram's horn, to summon the faithful. Later, they were called to prayer by the ringing of a bell (*naqus*), after the fashion of Christians. The adoption of another practice—the muezzin's call—may reflect a desire on the part of Muslims to distinguish themselves from Jews and Christians.

The choice of Friday as the day for the great prayer also likely resulted from a dialectic between Jewish prayer and the polemic that targeted the Medina Jews. There is reason to believe that the Friday midday prayer (*ṣalat al-jum'a*) was not established in Mecca prior to the *hijra*, as the Muslim minority in that town had yet to acquire sufficient status between the beginning of Muhammad's predication in 610 and the town's takeover in 630. According to Muslim tradition, the Muslims of Medina had observed that the Jews and Christians both had a great weekly gathering and they wanted to imitate them.

The choice of Friday as the principal day of Muslim prayer has been a topic of considerable research in Islamic studies. Building upon studies by Carl Heinrich Becker and Arent Jan Wensinck, Shlomo Dov Goitein explains this choice by reference to the fact that Friday was market day in Medina, as well as the day when the Jews prepared for Shabbat. As was the custom on market days, the crowds that gathered consisted not just of local inhabitants, but also of people from neighboring villages. The presence of these crowds, among them many Medina Jews, fueled hopes that the message of Islam would reach the ears of more people on Fridays than on other days. The link between commercial activity and Friday prayer is evident in the verses that mention the latter:

> O you who believe, when proclamation is made for prayer on the day of assembly, hasten to remembrance of God and leave [your] trading. That is better for you, did you but know. And when prayer is ended, disperse in the land to seek some of God's bounty and remember God much so that you may prosper. When they see merchandise or some diversion, they scatter to it and leave you standing. Say, "What is with God is better than diversion and merchandise. God is the best of providers!" (Q. 62:9–11)

As these verses show, Islam's Friday day of prayer differs markedly from Shabbat, which was a day of rest. Trade and all other activity were interrupted only during the hour of prayer. Afterward the faithful were called upon to return to their affairs: "Disperse in the land to seek some of God's bounty."

The choice of Friday prayer clearly reflects an awareness of the existence of a Jewish community, as well as a desire to differentiate oneself from that community by substituting Friday for Shabbat. Unlike the latter, it would not be a day of rest and would serve to attract that community by its convenient timing.

Let us now consider the controversy regarding the direction of prayer. This is mentioned in two passages in the Qur'an, both resonant of discord. If one merely relies on the verses themselves, it is difficult to determine against whom their invectives are directed. For this, one must turn to the commentaries on the Qur'an, which point to an anti-Jewish polemic. The first of these passages states: "Unto God belong the East and the West. Wherever you turn, there is the face of God" (Q. 2:115). While the original meaning of the verse is not especially clear, the commentators understood it as meaning that, in contrast to what the Jews claimed, the direction of prayer was of secondary importance. Later in the same sura one finds verses of more obvious polemical intent:

> The fools among the people will say, "What has turned them away from the *qibla* which they used to observe?" Say: "Unto God belong the East and the West. He guides those whom He wishes to a straight path" [...] And We fixed the *qibla* that you used to observe only to recognize those who would follow the messenger [Muhammad] from those who turn on their heels [...]. We see you turning your face about in the sky and so We make you turn to a *qibla* that will please you. Turn your face towards the Sacred Mosque. Wherever you may be, turn your faces towards it." (Q. 2:143–144)

The evidence provided by these obscure verses is no more than piecemeal. The tradition nevertheless interpreted them as evidence of an enduring polemic between Muhammad and the Jews of Medina regarding the appropriate direction of prayer. At the time when Muhammad was forming ties with the town's Jews—a period of roughly one and a half years following his arrival there—the Prophet ordered his followers to pray in the direction of Jerusalem (this is why the town is called *ula l-qiblatayn,* "the first of two directions of prayer [in Islam]"). Although we do not know which groups are referred to by the words "to distinguish those who follow the Messenger from those who turn on their heels," it is clear that a condemnation is intended. The commentators see it as an allusion to the period following Muhammad's break with the Jews. In fact, the preceding period of rapprochement was characterized by the adoption of Jewish-originated ideas, rituals, laws, and customs. In the period of separation that followed, there arose a desire to create a religion quite distinct from that of the Jews, as is suggested by the well-known ḥadith, "Do not resemble the Jews or the Christians" (*la tashabbahu bi-l-yahud wa-l-nasara*), and another: "Show your disagreement with the Jews" (*khalifu l-yahud*).[5] In other words, Muslim precepts were altered so as to dispel their obvious links to Judaism and Christianity while also asserting the originality of the Muslim position, for nascent Islam saw the two religions that had preceded it as at once a source of inspiration and a threat to its identity. While the Jews and first Muslims prayed together in the direction of Jerusalem, later Muslims began to turn towards "the Lord's house" (*bayt Allah*) in Mecca. This decision in its own right illustrates the Muslims' desire to separate themselves from Judaism.

To round off the complex portrait of research regarding these polemical verses, reference must be made to an article by Uri Rubin, "The Direction of Prayer in Islam: On the History of a Conflict Between Rituals,"[6] in which Rubin expresses a view that diverges from prevailing opinion. Drawing on a new analysis of the ḥadith relating to this subject, he reverses the conventional order: it is not the desire for separation from the Jews that brought about the change of direction in prayer (from Jerusalem to Mecca); rather, it was this change that caused the rift between Muhammad and the Jews. Rubin also maintains that this change of *qibla* was part of a broader internal evolution within Islam, which saw the Kaʿba attaining a preponderant cultural role. In his view, this symbolized its radical break with the earlier religions of Judaism and Christianity. The fact of turning toward Syria and the land of Israel, however, was part of this. Mecca and Jerusalem were holy places before the advent of Islam; consequently, continuing to pray in the direction of Jerusalem for a year and a half after the *hijra* must be understood as more than a way of attracting Jews to Islam. According to Rubin, asserting the holiness of Jerusalem was essential for

Islam, not merely a strategy on the part of the Prophet after the *hijra*. In other words, an orientation toward Jerusalem was not a belated political maneuver undertaken by a newly imperial Islam, but rather a religious imperative dating from the time of Muhammad himself. The land of Israel, in general, and Jerusalem, in particular, occupy an absolutely central place in Judaism and Christianity, but these two religions were the cultural background out of which Islam arose. It is thus not astonishing that the latter, which laid claim to this heritage, should have inherited their geographic conceptions as well.

The Laws of Fasting

The pagans of the Arabian Peninsula practiced fasting before Islam, in the month of Rajab, which was made to correspond to the seventh month of the Muslim calendar. Many traditions confirm that the practice was in fact very widespread at this time, though we do not know for what cause or purpose. But whatever the circumstances, at the time of Islam's emergence, it was necessary to suppress this usage so as to confer upon Ramadan its status as the only month of fasting, a practice that would become a central component of Islam—indeed, one of the five pillars of the faith—in the course of Muhammad's stay in Medina.

One tradition holds that, upon his arrival in Medina, Muhammad observed the Jews fasting on "the tenth day of the first month" and asked them:

What is this day that you fast? They [the Jews] responded: "It's a great day on which God saved Moses and his people and drowned Pharaoh and his people. Moses thus fasted to thank God, therefore we fast as well." The Prophet Muhammad responded: "We are more worthy to lay claim to Moses than you!" Thus, he fasted that day and organized the fast.[7]

According to Muslim tradition, the Jews of Medina referred to their fast as 'Ashura—that is, the fast of the tenth day of the month of Muḥarram, which is the first month of the Muslim calendar. "'Ashura" derives from the root '-sh-r (ten), which scholars generally agree referred to the fast of Kippur, which as we know takes place on the tenth day of the month of Tishri—the seventh month of the year according to the Bible's reckoning (Leviticus 23:26), but the first month according to post-biblical Jewish tradition.

The reason given by Islam for designating this, the most important day of the Jewish calendar, for fasting was the desire to underscore the link between Muhammad and Moses; this despite the fact that, in the Torah, the fast of Kippur had no direct link with the exodus from Egypt but rather related to God's forgiveness following the episode of the Golden Calf.

As we have already seen, it was commonplace in Islamic tradition to justify the commandments of Islam by reference to the existence of similar commandments in the Jewish (or Christian) tradition. As we shall see below, the pilgrimage (ḥajj), which is another of the five pillars of Islam, is associated with Abraham. In these two cases, the notion that Muhammad was closely associated with the biblical prophets (Moses or Abraham) led Islam to adopt an ancient practice. The fundamental postulate was the same in both cases: to the degree that the prophet Muhammad saw himself as the successor to the biblical prophets, commandments and practices advocated by them should properly be adopted by ancient Islam.

Yet this link to Moses is not the only explanation for the establishment of the fast of 'Ashura. According to other traditions, it commemorated the day Noah exited the arc or reflected the fact that, before the advent of Islam, it was customary in Muhammad's tribe, the Quraysh, to fast on that day. We are doubtless here confronted with a process similar to that which we observed at work in regards to the direction of prayer: a fast day was first established on the model of Yom Kippur, underscoring the link with Moses; efforts were then made to associate this image with a more universal figure like Noah; and it was finally presented as a purely Arab practice with no links to Judaism. The differentiation from Judaism was expressed in the cancellation of the fast of 'Ashura and its transformation into an elective practice, while another fast—that of Ramadan—was established. Yet the day of 'Ashura would be recuperated by Shi'i worship, where to this day it commemorates the memory of the martyrdom of the third Imam, Ḥusayn, a grandson of the Prophet killed at Karbala by Umayyad forces. In Shi'i consciousness, Muhammad's early establishment of the fast of 'Ashura in Medina thus takes on an additional meaning, anticipating the holy history of the Imams.

Islam conferred on Ramadan a distinctly Muslim character that marked it as definitively different from the fasts of religions that preceded it. The process by which this happened follows the generally acknowledged chronology of the revelations as they are presented in the chapters of the Qur'an. For according to the latter, the verse prescribing the fast of Ramadan (Q. 2:185) was revealed to Muhammad in the second year of the *hijra* (that is, the year 624), a date that marks the end of Muhammad's efforts to form ties with the Jews of Medina. It came as a sign of the widening gulf separating Jews and Muslims.

Although the establishment of Ramadan apparently signaled a complete break with Judaism, several considerations suggest the two continued to be linked to one another. Goitein drew attention to the resemblance between Islam and Judaism, both of which associated the commandment to fast with the revelation of Holy Scripture. According to Islam: "[It is] the month of Ramadan, in which the Qur'an was sent down as guidance to the people and clear proofs of the guidance and of the salvation . . ." (Q. 2:185).

It is not possible, according to Goitein, that this association between the revelation of the divine word and the month of fasting came out of thin air. According to the Midrash, the fast of Kippur falls precisely on the date when Moses came down from Sinai with the ten tablets of the Law, after forgiveness had been granted for the sin of the Golden Calf (that is, three times forty days after the feast of Shavu'ot, when Moses received the first tablets of the Law).[8]

Echoes of Jewish law as it is expressed in the first collection of post-biblical laws, or Mishna, may even be identified in various details in the Qur'an prescribing how the fast was to be conducted. Consider this example: During Ramadan, the Qur'an authorizes food to be eaten between dusk and dawn, defined as the moment when one can first make out colors: "Eat and drink until the white thread is distinct to you from the black thread at dawn" (Q. 2:187). Many scholars have underscored this passage's resemblance to the definition supplied by the Mishna, famous for occurring at the very beginning of the first treatise: "From what time may one recite the Shema in the morning? From the time that one can distinguish between blue and white" (Mishna, *Berakhot* I, 2).

Such similarities between the two texts must not lead us to neglect their differences. In both cases, it is true, the ability to discern color is what allows one to determine the onset of dawn. In the Mishna, however, this relates to prayer, whereas in the Qur'an, it has to do with fasting. In the Mishna, the colors in question are blue and white (as in the *tallit*) whereas, in the Qur'an, they are white and black. It is impossible to know whether the resemblance here is purely accidental or the result of borrowing.[9]

On the other hand, the Qur'an authorizes believers who are unable to fully observe the commandment to fast to make up for it at a later date: "Those of you who are sick or on a journey [should fast] a number of other days" (Q. 2:184). In post-Qur'anic literature this precept is extended to other cases: to women who are menstruating or have just given birth, and being thus impure, cannot fast for the entire duration of Ramadan. Such a dispensation can also be found in the Bible and Talmudic literature. The biblical precedent is that of the "Second" or substitution Passover (*Pessaḥ Sheni*): "If any man of you or of your posterity shall be unclean by reason of a dead body or be in a journey afar off, yet he shall keep the Passover unto the Lord" (Numbers 9:10). The solution put forward is to celebrate the holiday exactly one month from the day (the 15th of Iyar) instead of on the original date (the 15th of Nisan). In the Mishna, an analogous solution is offered for missed prayer: whoever forgoes one of the three daily prayers may under well-defined conditions make up for it at the time of the next prayer.

Although the domains in which this regulation applies are not identical—in one case fasting, in the other Passover and prayer—one cannot help but note the similarity in the solutions proposed to the believer who fails to perform his religious duty in a timely fashion. One might of course claim that this resemblance is fortuitous, but in the Jewish environment in which Islam emerged, it is quite possible that such regulations passed from Judaism into nascent Islam.

Dietary Laws

Apart from the fact that Islam and Judaism share dietary prohibitions regarding certain animals, their resemblance in this area is minimal. The dietary laws of Islam—at least at the stratum reflected in the Qur'an—are simple and few in number, with only a short list of proscribed animals: "O you who believe, eat the good things that We have provided for your sustenance and be grateful to God if you worship Him. He has forbidden for you carrion, blood, the flesh of the pig, and anything that has been dedicated to any other than God . . ." (Q. 2:172–173; see also Q. 5:3–5, which contains a few more prohibitions; and Q. 6:145–146). This is in no way comparable to the lists supplied by the Bible, which enumerate many species of animal as prohibited from consumption (Leviticus 11:1–47; Deuteronomy 14:3–21). The common denominator between the two religions is their prohibition of pork, blood, and carrion.

As is also the case of Christian polemics against Judaism,[10] the Qur'an interprets the abundance of prohibitions specific to Judaism as a punishment imposed on the Jews: "For those who are Jews, We have forbidden everything with claws; and of cattle and sheep We have forbidden the fat of them save that carried by their backs or the intestines or what is mixed with bone. This is how we penalized them for their disobedience. We speak the truth" (Q. 6:146). And, in a similar vein: "Because of wrong-doing on the part of the Jews, We have forbidden them good things which had been lawful to them; and because of their turning many from God's way . . . We have prepared for those of them who do not believe a painful torment" (Q. 4:160).

The notion that most of the dietary restrictions imposed on the Jews were not original, but rather applied later in their history as punishment for their sins is rooted in another verse mentioning Jacob (under the name of Israel). It claims that, in the time of this patriarch, all foods were permitted for consumption. "All food was lawful for the children of Israel apart from that which Israel [=Jacob] forbade to himself before the Torah was sent down" (Q. 3:93). Unlike the verses quoted above, this verse does not present the dietary prohibitions as a punishment imposed upon the Jews, but merely alludes to the fact that these prohibitions did not always exist. The restriction expressed by the words "apart from that which Israel forbade to himself" seemingly refers to the prohibition of the sciatic nerve that followed Jacob's struggle with the angel. At the end of the struggle, which lasted until daybreak, Jacob's hip was dislocated: "Therefore the Children of Israel eat not of the sinew which shrank, which is upon the hollow of the thigh, unto this day, because he touched the hollow of Jacob's thigh in the sinew that shrank" (Genesis 32:33). The Qur'an does not mention this biblical episode, the only echo of which is to be found in this prohibition on consuming the sciatic nerve. It is interesting to note that Jacob does not appear in this Qur'anic verse under the name of Jacob, but rather under the name Israel given him by the angel against whom he struggled (Genesis 32:29). The use of "Israel" to refer to Jacob can only be found on one other occasion in the Qur'an (Q. 19:58). In the sixteen other occasions on which he appears, he is referred to by the more common name of Ya'qub (=Jacob).

Another point of commonality between Islam and Judaism is the severity with which both condemn the consumption of animals offered in sacrifice to idols. Thus: "Forbidden to you are: carrion, blood, the flesh of the pig; anything on which [the name of] any other than God has been invoked . . ." (Q. 5:3). This prohibition is very prominent in the Talmud. One also encounters it in primitive Christianity, which, at the Council of

Jerusalem, forbade "meats sacrificed to the idols" as well as blood and strangled animals (*Acts of the Apostles* 15:29).

In his book, *The Jewish Foundation of Islam*, Charles Torrey writes that Muhammad's intention was originally to imitate Jewish dietary laws, but that the "conditions and customs in Arabia necessitated some differences . . . [and] the laws of Israel are now superseded by the Muslim enactments."[11] Whatever the case, dietary prohibitions and the laws that encoded them—for example, the rules governing ritual slaughter and those concerning the non-dietary uses of animals prohibited from consumption—continued to develop in parallel in Judaism and Islam, as we shall see in the final chapter.[12]

The Calendar and the Embolismic Year

Many calendars represent an effort to harmonize the solar cycle (which defines a year consisting of 365 and one quarter days, and on which the climatic seasons depend) and the lunar cycle (which defines months consisting of 29 or 30 days, which means that one "year" consisting of twelve lunar months contains 354 days). The Romans and, after them, the Christian West opted for a basically solar calendar with 30- or 31-day months that in no way depended on the lunar cycle. The Jews, however, had to take divergent biblical commands into account: the months (and thus holidays falling on a certain day of the month) had to be determined in accordance with the new moon; but these same holidays also had to fall within specific agricultural seasons (the holiday of Pessaḥ, in particular, had to take place in the spring). The result was a complex science by means of which, over the course of nineteen-year cycles, a thirteenth month was added every two or three years to prevent the seasons from "losing" ten days with each passing year.

The Muslim calendar is strictly lunar: the month of Ramadan, like all other months, moves from one year to the next, passing from summer to winter in the space of a decade. Moreover, Year 1 of the Muslim calendar is that of the *hijra*—that is, the year of the Prophet's flight from Mecca and "emigration" (*hijra*) to Medina. Establishing a calendar was thus a matter of conferring meaning upon the long-term of universal history while at the same time meeting the short-term exigencies of everyday life.

The establishment of the Islamic calendar was also the occasion for a polemic against various groups: first against the pagan Arabs in whose midst Islam first emerged, and then against other religions, particularly Judaism. By detaching themselves from so deeply rooted a usage as the calendar, the first Muslims expressed their desire to distinguish themselves from other communities. According to tradition, their new *hijri* calendar was established by the second caliph, 'Umar ibn al-Khattab (caliph from 634 to 644).

In the Qur'an, controversy over the calendar mainly centers on the practice of adding a thirteenth, intercalary month:

> The number of the months with God is twelve, [laid down] in God's decree on the day that He created the heavens and the earth [. . .]. Intercalation (*al-nasi'*) is a further unbelief (*ziyada fi-l-kufr*) by which those who disbelieve are led astray. They allow it one year and forbid it another year to level up the number of what God has made sacred and to allow what God has forbidden. (Q. 9:36–37)

Though the Qur'an does not formally recommend that it be forbidden, it presents this intercalation of an additional month as a sign of infidelity to the Divine Law established at the dawn of creation. The question thus arises: against whom is this polemic directed? Classical commentators past and present generally answer by pointing to the pagan Arab context: the Arabs of the time agreed that certain months of the year were sacred and should be devoted to pilgrimage; for reasons of comfort, however, some tribes manipulated the calendar by adding months. It would nevertheless be very surprising were Jews not the target of this polemic, for they are the only group known to have added an intercalary month (a practice that continues to this day). Moreover, the sura in question (9, or *al-Tawba*) dates from the end of the Medina period. According to many scholars, it even comes last in the order of Qur'anic revelation, thus belonging to a time when Muhammad's split with the Jews seems to have been consummated once and for all. Throughout this sura, and especially in the verses that adjoin those concerning the intercalation of the month, Jews and Christians are criticized with particular virulence. A few examples: the famous verse 29 on the *jizya* (poll tax, tribute) lays down the Qur'anic position as to the inferior status of the "people of the book" (a term that encompasses Jews and Christians as well as, at times, Zoroastrians) under Islamic government. In the subsequent parts of the verse, it is stated that force must be used against them should they not pay their tribute: "Fight from among the people who have been given the Scripture [. . .] until they pay the tribute readily, having been humbled."[13] In the verse that follows (Q. 9:30), the Jews and Christians are rebuked for their inadequate faith in monotheism, on the grounds that they attribute a son to God: "The Jews say, 'Uzayr is the son of God'; and the Christians say: 'Christ is the son of God.' That is what they say in their mouths, conforming to what was said by those who disbelieved before them. God confound them. How they are embroiled in lies!" (9:30).[14] Other accusations are levelled against them in the verses that follow, such as verse 32: "They wish to extinguish God's light with their mouths but God refuses [to do] anything other than to perfect His light, even though the unbelievers dislike that." Or verse 34: "Many of the rabbis and monks (*al-aḥbar wa-l-ruhban*) consume people's possessions in vanity and bar [people] from God's way."

The verse regarding the intercalation of the month occurs in the exact middle of these fierce polemics. The context thus seems to be anti-Jewish and anti-Christian. Remarkably, however, no Muslim religious source to my knowledge justified prohibiting the intercalary month in the name of opposing Judaism. Instead, it was Muslim astronomers who were to mention the influence of Judaism on pre-Islamic Arab habits in what concerned the intercalary month. The famous scholar Abu Rayḥan al-Biruni (d. 1048) put it thus: "They [the Arabs] learned the intercalation of the month from the Jews who lived in their neighborhood and this more than two centuries before the *hijra* and they set about adopting this Jewish practice by adding a month between the [lunar] year and the solar year."[15] On reading this account, one notes that the influence of Jewish sources on the Arabs was indeed the result of exchanges between two communities living side by side, both before and after the advent of Islam.

Conclusion

These examples regarding halakhic subjects indeed confirm that the relations between Judaism and the Qur'anic message were as close and complex in what is known as the Medina period as they were in the classical era. At once proximate and remote, these relations show that, while Muslim scholars alluded to biblical and post-biblical texts and adopted Jewish ideas, they simultaneously endeavored to distinguish themselves from Judaism. An expression that perfectly summarizes this dialectic may be found in verse Q. 2:143, which occurs towards the end of the verses regarding the *qibla* discussed above: "Thus We have made you a moderate community (*ummatan wasatan*)." For all commentators, this key verse designates Islam as the "middle way," the religion that, in contrast to Judaism and Christianity, never tends toward extremes. The Judaism that the first Muslims knew in Medina was immediately seen as a restrictive religion. According to the Qur'an, many of the commandments that the Jews had to obey—for example, dietary prohibitions much stricter than those practiced by Muslims and, of course, Christians—were imposed by God as punishment for their sins.

V

The Qur'anic Sources of *Dhimma*

THE QUR'AN does not explicitly address the issue of the legal status of Jews or of the followers of other religions under the reign of Islam. This issue did not arise until the post-Qur'anic period, when the emergence of a Muslim Empire brought together many religious minorities under the aegis of Islam. It was necessary then to define the rules and conditions that would allow them to live in the shadow of Islam. Although the Qur'an does not explicitly address this subject, it nevertheless contains a not inconsiderable number of verses that reflect the inferiority attributed to Jews and served as a pretext for their low legal status. The first of these verses puts it as follows:

> Humiliation (*al-dhilla*) will be stamped on them wherever they are found, unless [they grasp] a rope from God and a rope from the people. They have incurred anger from God and wretchedness (*al-maskana*) will be stamped upon them. That is because they used to disbelieve in the signs of God and slayed the prophets without right. That is because they were rebellious and used to transgress. (Q. 3:112)

As this verse makes clear, the condition of the people of the book was marked by continuous humiliation (*al-dhilla*). To this was added their wretchedness (*maskana*), which the Qur'an justified by reference to the two great sins of which the People of the Book were guilty: their failure to recognize divine signs and their murder of the prophets who were sent to them. The verse also mentions exceptions for whom humiliation does not obtain: "those who were protected by a link with God or men." These are the Jews and Christians who, in the earliest days of Islam, were protected by alliances concluded with the Arab tribes. Yet the Qur'an does not forbid humiliating them; it merely orders that they be protected, as demonstrated by the well-known Qur'an commentator Isma'il b. 'Umar ibn Kathir's (d. 1373) commentary on this verse. He shows that the basic principles of the laws of protection that subsequently developed in Islam were anchored in the verse. God thus established that they—the Jews—would always be in humiliation and subjection (*al-dhilla wa-l-ṣaghar*) in all places they find themselves have no protection other than through the intercession of their "link with God"—that is, God's protection (*al-dhimma*) and the payment of tribute (*jizya*). Their "link with men," meanwhile, will ensure their security (*aman*)."[1]

The "*jizya* verse" is perhaps even better known:

> Fight from among the people who have been given the Scripture those who do not believe in God and the Last Day and do not forbid that which God and His messenger have forbidden and who do not follow the religion of truth, until they pay the tribute (*jizya*) readily (*'an yadin*), having been humbled. (Q. 9:29–30)[2]

This verse has received the attention of many scholars and given rise to a large number of studies seeking to shed light on its general context and the specific expressions it contains. For example, what is the meaning of the vague expression *'an yadin*, which Alan Jones translates as "readily" and Arthur Arberry translates as "out of the hand"? This expression, which literally means "by means of" or "by [way of] the hand," has been interpreted in various other ways as well. The strictest of these interpretations claims that, when paying the *jizya*, the non-Muslim who enjoyed protection had to solemnly place his hand next to that of the tax collector in acknowledgement of his own inferiority and subjection to Islam. Another interpretation—one that describes an ideal, nay utopian situation of propinquity between the Muslim and his protégé—understands the expression *'an yadin* to mean "as far as his means allow."[3] There have in fact been periods and places under Islamic government in which the *jizya* was seen as a progressive tax to be levied in proportion to the protégé's resources.[4]

Whatever the case, an examination of this verse and the preceding one (as well as all the other verses critical of the Jews, which we saw in Chapter 2) shows that, in legal and other terms, the Qur'an played an important role in promoting discrimination against the Jews. Yet the inferiority and abasement of the Jews and other people of the book occupies just one side of the coin, the other being an assertion of Islam's religious and cultural superiority. The foundations of this principle are laid by many verses in the Qur'an. For example: "[It is] He who has sent His messenger with the guidance and the religion of truth to cause it to prevail over all [other] religion, even though the polytheists dislike that" (Q. 9:33; cf. also Q. 48:28 and Q. 61:9). And: "Those who seek some religion other than Islam (=submission), it will not be accepted from them—they will be among the losers in the world to come" (Q. 3:85). This idea was extensively developed in the literature of ḥadith and is confirmed by many traditions attributed to the prophet Muhammad—for example, the very famous tradition according to which "Islam is supreme and nothing is superior to it (*al-islam ya'lu wa-la yu'la 'alayhi*)." One may find other traditional teachings that more particularly specify the superiority of Islam vis-à-vis the revealed religions that preceded it, specifically Judaism and Christianity. For example: "Be careful not to glorify either Judaism or Christianity (*la turfa'anna fikum la yahudiyya wa-la naṣraniyya*)."

Yet it was only with the "Pact of 'Umar," several generations after Islam first emerged that this ideological stance, underscored by the Qur'anic verses and prophetic teachings cited here (together with many others), attained its definitive legal form.

The Pact of 'Umar

The collection of legal measures known as the "Pact of 'Umar" is generally considered to be the ideological and legal foundation that defined Islam's relations with the People of the Book. It is traditionally attributed to the caliph 'Umar ibn al-Khattab (ruler from 634 to 644) but was probably developed during the reign of Umayyad caliph 'Umar b. 'Abd al-'Aziz (ruler from 717 to 720), who was known for his hostility toward Jews and Christians. It consists of a collection of discriminatory laws defining the legal status of the People of the Book—that is, the Jews, Christians, and other peoples living in Islamic lands, such as the *majus* ("mages"), or Zoroastrians, who succeeded in having the Avesta recognized as a sacred book even though it does not fall under Abrahamic monotheism. These People of the Book were accorded the status of *dhimmis*—that is, subject minorities "protected" by the Islamic government, in contrast to the pagans, who had no choice but conversion, death or, at best, slavery.

More specifically, all versions of the Pact of 'Umar mention Christians only, and the various religious restrictions it lays out—for example, the prohibition on building churches and monasteries, ringing bells to call to prayer, and holding noisy ceremonies—apply only to Christianity. This doubtless reflects the fact that Christians were the majority population in the territories conquered by Islam. These restrictions were nevertheless extended to Jews and Zoroastrians as well, so that everything the document says about Christians applies to these groups as well.

Over the centuries, many decrees were added to the Pact of 'Umar, among them one attributed to the Abbasid caliph al-Mutawwakil (who reigned from 847 to 861). It faithfully reflects the position of all Muslim legal scholars, whatever their school, in what concerns the religions of the Book. However, rigorous study of Muslim legal literature on those considered protégés (*dhimmis*) enables us to fully grasp the relations between this legal theory properly so called and its practical implementation. This allows us to ask: did these *dhimma* laws reflect real situations, or were they merely the description of an ideal that was never perfectly realized? This question has no simple answer. Claude Cahen noted: "It would appear that these regulations were never respected for any length of time (whence their repetition by pietistic sovereigns) and it is even doubtful whether there was any real desire to apply them outside of Baghdad and the great Islamic centers."[5]

Here is the text of the Pact:[6]

"'Abd al-Rahman b. Ghanm related: When 'Umar ibn al-Khattab, may God be pleased with him, made peace with the Christian inhabitants of Syria, we wrote to him as follows:

In the name of God, the Merciful and Compassionate. This is a letter to the servant of God, 'Umar, the Commander of the Faithful, from the Christians of such-and-such city.

When you came against us, we asked you for a guarantee of security (*aman*) for ourselves, our offspring, our property and the people of our religious community (*milla*) and we undertook the following obligations toward you, namely:

- We shall not build in our cities or in their vicinity new monasteries, churches, hermitages, or monks' cells, nor shall we repair, by night or day, any of them that have fallen into ruin or which are located in the quarters of the Muslims.
- We shall keep our gates wide open for passersby and travelers.
- We shall provide three days' food and lodging to any Muslims who pass our way.
- We shall not give shelter in our churches or in our homes to any spy nor hide him from the Muslims.
- We shall not teach our children the Qur'an.
- We shall not hold public religious ceremonies.
- We shall not seek to proselytize anyone.
- We shall not prevent any of our kin from embracing Islam if they so desire.
- We shall show deference to the Muslims and shall rise from our seats when they wish it.
- We shall not attempt to resemble the Muslims in any way with regard to their dress, as, for example, with the *qalansuwa* [a conical cap], the turban, footwear or parting of the hair.
- We shall not speak as they do nor shall we adopt their *kunyas* [honorific bynames].
- We shall not ride on saddles.
- We shall not wear swords or bear weapons of any kind or even carry them on our persons.
- We shall not engrave Arabic inscriptions on our seals.
- We shall not sell alcoholic beverages.

- We shall dress in our traditional fashion wherever we may be and we shall bind the *zunnar* [a distinctive belt] around our waists.
- We shall not display our crosses or our books anywhere in the roads or markets of the Muslims.
- We shall only beat the clappers in our churches very quietly.
- We shall not raise our voices in our church services, nor in the presence of Muslims.
- We shall not go outside on Palm Sunday or Easter nor shall we raise our voices in our funeral processions.
- We shall not display lights in any of the roads of the Muslims or in the marketplaces.
- We shall not come near them with our funeral processions [or: we shall not bury our dead near the Muslims].
- We shall not take slaves who have been allotted to the Muslims.
- We shall not build our homes higher than theirs.

[Amendment Clause] When I brought the letter to 'Umar, may God be pleased with him, he added: "We shall not strike any Muslim."

Such are the conditions to which we have subscribed, we and our co-religionists, and in exchange for which we receive protection. If it should happen that we contravene a few of these commitments for which we are answerable in our persons, we will no longer have right to *dhimma* and we will be liable to the punishments reserved for rebels and the seditious.

'Umar ibn al-Khattab responded to 'Abd al-Rahman ibn Ghamm: "'Approve their request' but not before adding to what they have subscribed to the two following conditions I impose upon them: 'They will not be able to purchase individuals taken prisoner by Muslims. He who will have deliberately struck a Muslim will no longer benefit from any guarantee from this pact.'"

As one can see, these laws reflect various aspects of the relations between Islam and its subject populations: a prohibition on building places of worship or restoring those that have been destroyed; an obligation to provide Muslims with lodging and a prohibition on harboring spies and enemies of Islam; a prohibition on other religions engaging in ostentatious displays; a prohibition on riding a saddled mount (which amounts to forbidding the use of any noble mount, such as the horse); and a prohibition on bearing arms and the obligation to wear specific clothing allowing protégés to be distinguished from their Muslim patrons. In exchange for these restrictions and payment of the *jizya*, the protégés' lives were spared and they were permitted to practice their religion.

There is agreement among scholars that the restrictions imposed by the Pact of 'Umar were influenced by Byzantine and Sassanian law, which the Muslims encountered after the first wave of Muslim conquests outside of the Arabian Peninsula swept over regions belonging to these two rival empires. Each of them practiced a state religion corresponding to that of the majority population (Christianity in the one case, Zoroastrianism in the other) and recognized tolerated religious minorities—in particular, Jews. This tolerance, however, was accompanied by stringent restrictions (such as those enumerated in the Theodosian Code of 404 CE) and came at the price of sporadic persecution, as under the reign of Justinian in the Byzantine case (553 CE) and that of Yazdegerd II in its Persian counterpart (456 CE).

A Long Codification

Islamic legislation regarding the status of Jews as *dhimmis* was not put into writing until two centuries after the advent of Islam. It is reflected in the literature of the four legal schools of Sunni Islam, as well as in Shi'i legal writings. These codes did not originally devote a section to the legal rules concerning *dhimmis*, however, but rather dispersed relevant articles under various other headings. In *Kitab al-mabsut*, a legal code for the ḥanafite school (one of the four schools of Sunni Islam) written by Shams al-Din al-Sarakhsi (d. 1090), one thus sees that the question of whether one may marry *dhimmis* is contained in a subchapter of the treatise on marriage (*kitab al-nikaḥ*). The commercial rules contained in the treatise on sales (*kitab al-bay'*), meanwhile, include a chapter on trading with *dhimmis*. The same holds for the codes of the other Sunni schools. And the great Shi'i codifier, Abu Ja'far al-Tusi (d. 1067), follows a similar path in his two works of jurisprudence, *Tahdhib al-aḥkam* ("Rectification of the Statutes") and *al-Istibsar fi ma khtulifa min al-akhbar* ("Reflections upon the Disputed Traditions").

Legislation concerning protégés was not systematized until the late Middle Ages, a process notably illustrated by Ibn Qayyim al-Jawziyya's sprawling monograph (d. 1350), *Aḥkam ahl al-dhimma* ("The Laws Concerning Dhimmis"). Drily and concisely formulated by the Pact of 'Umar, the discriminatory rules governing *dhimmis* are there presented in more detailed and developed form.[7] This legal literature debates the issue of whether the Pact of 'Umar is in need of revision and, if so, under what conditions. The dominant position of classical Muslim legal writing, however, is that the Pact is valid across generations and must be retained.

Between Theory and Reality

There is no question that the terms of the Pact of 'Umar undergird the attitudes generally adopted toward Jews and other minorities over the course of Muslim history. In order to form an idea of the actual situation of Jews living in the shadow of Islam, however, one must determine as precisely as possible how these laws were applied from one place and time to the next. The role played by each scholar's subjectivity must also be taken into account, in so far as it might lead to privileging certain aspects over others to create an overall vision of the legal situation of Jews under Islam.

Bernard Lewis, one of the greatest scholars of Islam of the twentieth and early twenty-first centuries, opens his book *The Jews of Islam* with this insightful remark:

> Two stereotypes dominate most of what has been written on tolerance and intolerance in the Islamic world. The first depicts a fanatical warrior, an Arab horseman riding out of the desert with a sword in one hand and the Qur'an in the other, offering his victims the choice between the two. This picture, made famous by Edward Gibbon in his *Decline and Fall of the Roman Empire*, is not only false but impossible [...]. The other image, almost equally preposterous, is that of an interfaith, interracial utopia, in which men and women belonging to different races, professing different creeds, lived side by side in a golden age of unbroken harmony, enjoying equality of rights and of opportunities, and toiling together for the advancement of civilization. To put the two stereotypes in Jewish terms, in one version classical Islam was like modern America, only better; in the other it was like Hitler's Germany, only worse, if such can be imagined. Both images are

of course wildly distorted; yet both contain, as stereotypes often do, some elements of truth.[8]

Together with Marc Cohen in the book cited above and Michel Abitbol in his book, *Le Passé d'une discorde: juifs et Arabes du VIIᵉ siècle à nos jours*,[9] Bernard Lewis sees the history of Jews under Islamic domination as repeatedly oscillating between these two extremes. The history of the Jews under Islam, in other words, is not monolithic. The historian who seeks the truth has no license to generalize; each place and each period needs to be researched in its own right.

There is no question that the history of the Jews under Islam contains situations in which the Jews suffered discrimination and lived under conditions more bitter than those imposed by the Pact of 'Umar. Bat Ye'or gives a great many examples of this, and one might add others.[10] Nevertheless, without wishing to minimize the misfortunes and persecutions that over the course of their history rained down on Jews in the lands of Islam, it is difficult to adopt either of these extreme positions. When Muslim authorities concluded that some restriction imposed on the *dhimmis* was not being observed strictly enough, they were in the habit of publishing the Pact of 'Umar in full and reminding the latter of their duty to observe it scrupulously. Yet rare were the cases in which an entire Jewish community was made to suffer as a result of one or several of its members failing to observe the Pact.

From Modernity to Fundamentalism

Finally, it must be noted that *dhimma* was officially abolished in nearly all Muslim states: first, between 1839 and 1856, in the Egypt of Mehmet Ali and throughout the Ottoman Empire in the context of a set of modernizing reforms (*tanzimat*) encompassing Turkey, Iraq, Yemen, Tunisia, Syria, and other countries; and subsequently in Morocco (1912) under the French Protectorate. Since their constitutions were not Islamic, none of these countries reestablished *dhimma* at the moment of independence. Among Islamic countries in which non-Muslim communities reside, only Iran still applies *dhimma*, and that under a form rather different from that of classical Islam. We will return to this issue in the following chapter.

Today, references to the *dhimma* are rather uncommon outside the sphere of political ideology. In the anti-Jewish discourse of some contemporary Islamic authorities, it is repeatedly claimed that Jews have no right to dominate Muslims at any time or place. In their eyes, the sovereignty of the State of Israel—where Muslims for the first time in the history of Islam find themselves under Jewish domination—thus constitutes an intolerable anomaly. Indeed, not only do Jews have no right to dominate Muslims, but the contrary should be the case, as it has throughout history, for Islam must dominate all other religions. As the ḥadith quoted above teaches: "Islam is superior and nothing can be superior to it." Among Islamists, and likewise among those who stir fears of a conquering Islam, the *dhimma* are more a figment of discourse than an actual reality.

VI

The Place of Judaism and the Jews in Twelver Shiʿism

GIVEN THAT Sunnism and Shiʿism are largely based on the same religious sources—first and foremost, the Qurʾan—one might well expect that their theological and legal attitudes toward Jews and their religion would be similar. In fact, the two great branches of Islam do in many respects overlap in their attitude towards Judaism, particularly in what concerns the positive and negative aspects of Jews and their religion, and this in both ancient and more recent times.

Despite the similarity of their positions vis-à-vis Jews and other Peoples of the Book,[1] several specifically Shiʿi conceptions relating to the Jews and Judaism may be identified in two areas of religious life. The first is that of the law, which is based on theological considerations, a domain to which only a small handful of specialists have until now given particular attention.[2] The main question that arises is the following: should the People of the Book be considered as ritually impure (*najis*)? In Shiʿi legal literature, this question has certain implications, particularly in what concerns the consumption of food (especially animals ritually slaughtered by Jews and Christians) and the possibility of marrying the latter's women.

The second area in which Shiʿism presents specific conceptions vis-à-vis Jews and their religion is that of doctrine. Here, the Shiʿi attitude is almost diametrically opposed to that found in the legal context: in multiple traditions, one finds the Shiʿa identified as the people of Israel or, more guardedly, the descendants of Israel are presented as being the prototype for Shiʿi Muslims. It is often surprising to find this approach in Shiʿi discourse, as it is strongly reminiscent of the traditional Christian attitude that consisted in seeing Christianity as the "True Israel" (*Verus Israel*). There is nevertheless considerable evidence for it.[3]

The Impurity of the *ahl al-kitab*

The controversy dividing Sunnis and Shiʿi over this question is based on the same Qurʾanic verses, of which the most important is: "O you who believe, the polytheists (*mushrikun*) are unclean. Let them not approach the Sacred Mosque (*al-masjid al-ḥaram*) after this year of theirs" (Q. 9:28).

In the exegesis of these verses, two major strains may be discerned. The first, which is based on the context of the preceding verses, holds that the term *mushrikun*, from the root *sh-r-k* that recurs 168 times in the Qurʾan and means "to associate" (almost always in the specific sense of "associating other divinities with Allah"), uniquely refers to the Meccan polytheists who were from that point on to be forbidden access to the sacred enclosure (the *ḥaram*) of Mecca. The second reading, by contrast, holds that the verse concerns all polytheists without exception, as well as all mosques.

The general tendency, moreover, is to include Jews and Christians under the term *mushrikun*, either because it is understood in a vague sense, or on the basis of the verse stating that the Jews made a divinity of ʿUzayr, just as the Christians made a divinity of Jesus (see above, p. 44–49). While most Sunni scholars limit this prohibition to Mecca, a "harder" tendency, tracing its roots to the Umayyad caliph discussed in the previous chapter, ʿUmar b. ʿAbd al-ʿAziz, extends it "to all mosques under any pretext."[4] By contrast, Sunni codifiers neither take the occurrence of "impurity" (najasa) in its literal sense, nor do they deduce from it that Jews or Christians are ritually impure. The impurity at issue pertains primarily to the rules of prayer and the need for being in a state of ritual purity before praying.

In Twelver Shiʿism, the dominant tendency in Qurʾanic exegesis, the literature of ḥadith, and legal writings cleaves firmly to the "hard" line mentioned above.[5] Studies of the many-volumed compendia of legal opinion, such as Muhammad Baqir al-Majlisi's (d. 1699) Biḥar al-anwar[6] and, much more recently, the multivolume work of the contemporary legal scholar, Ayatuʾllah Muhammad al-Ḥusayni Shirazi,[7] show a marked tendency to include Jews in the category of mushrikun and take the impurity imputed them by this verse in the literal, ritual sense. According to these sources, the latter must be seen as infidels and thus impure. Moreover, as in Sunnism, Shiʿism justifies this stance by expanding the meaning of the term shirk (to include "associationism," "polytheism," and "idolatry"). Nevertheless, the Shiʿi position on this question seems much more clear-cut. In developing their argument, Shiʿi scholars rely on Qurʾanic verses that call into question the Jews' monotheism. The work of Shirazi offers a summary detailing opinions expressed on this subject over the course of Shiʿi history.

According to al-Majlisi, the impurity of the people of the book must be understood as taking two forms: "spiritual impurity" (najasa maʿnawiyya),[8] resulting from "their fundamental wickedness and the corruption of their beliefs" (*khubth batini-him wa-su'i i'tiqadihim*);[9] and the concrete, physical impurity, often referred to as legal impurity (*najasa shar'iyya*),[10] or impurity as defined by legal prescriptions, that results from this spiritual impurity. In Shi'i jurisprudence, the issue is handled in several sub-chapters: Is it permitted to touch a member of the People of the Book or an object he has touched? Is it lawful to don clothing that he has earlier worn? Is one allowed to sleep in his bed? And so on.[11]

From the most "flexible" to the most "rigorous," scholars support their opinions by reference to traditions attributed to the Prophet and the Imams. Here are a few examples: The Imams Muhammad al-Baqir (d. ca. 731–32) and Ja'far al-Ṣadiq (d. 765) were asked: "Is it lawful to shake the hand of a Jew or a Christian?" They answered that the act was permitted if it took place "through an article of clothing, but if [the Jew or Christian] shakes your hand [directly], you must wash it."[12] Similarly, "while it is permitted to pray while wearing clothing bought from a Jew [without washing it first], yet, if it is bought from a Christian, it is only lawful to pray while wearing it after having washed it."[13] There nevertheless exist many other traditions going back to the Imams that convey other, more supple positions[14] allowing one, for example, to carry out ritual ablutions before prayer with a vessel touched by a Jew, use the water contained in such an object,[15] or wear clothing previously worn by a Zoroastrian (*majusi*).[16] The texts moreover sometimes reflect the disciples' perplexity vis-à-vis this tolerant attitude on the part of the Imams: "How can you be so indulgent (in what concerns the impurity of the people of the book) given that they drink wine and eat pork?" The Imams thus insisted on the need to be flexible.[17] Other traditions present the Imams as adopting a more demanding attitude toward themselves than toward their disciples. Imam al-Ṣadiq, for example, is said to have been asked by one of his disciples: "How must Muslims behave when they are at table and a Zoroastrian unexpectedly arrives? Must they invite him to share their meal?" He answered: "Personally, I do not sit down at table with a Zoroastrian but I dislike forbidding you something that you have the custom of doing in your country."[18]

Social Relations

Alongside prayer, the question of the Jews' impurity mainly bears upon the consumption of meat from animals they have ritually slaughtered and marriage with women from their community, themes already associated with one another in the Qurʾan:

> Permitted to you today are [all] good things. The food of those who have been given the Scripture is lawful for you and yours for them. [Permitted to you in marriage] are the chaste women of the believers and the chaste women of those who have been given the Scripture before you, if you give them your wages and if you live with them in wedlock, not in some loose arrangement or taking them as 'companions.' (Q. 5:5)

At first glance, these remarks, reinforced by other verses, explicitly allow both the consumption of food and marriage with women from the People of the Book. Yet these verses were the object of endless controversy among Sunni and Shiʿi scholars. While flexible and rigid stances can be found among both, the dominant tendency is different in the two branches of Islam. Among Sunni jurists, the main tendency is to show indulgence in two areas: it is lawful to consume animals slaughtered according to the ritual of the people of the book, and there is nothing wrong with marrying their women, although it is of course preferable to marry Muslim women.[19] As evidence of this, they point to the earliest history of Islam, which tells of the marriages of the Prophet Muhammad and his Companions with Jewish and Christian women.

In Shi'i law, the rigorist tendency dominates. Even indulgent scholars argue that preventative measures should be taken in contact with Jews and Christians and interpret Q. 5.5 in a way compatible with their position. Thus, the food that is permitted from the people of the book are such raw or "dry" foods as grains and greens. Their meat or any dishes cooked by them are off limites, for "meat and humid foods touched by them are impure and it is forbidden to consume them."[20] They justify (and in this are joined by some Sunnis) the prohibition on consuming food or animals ritually slaughtered by Jews and Christians by noting that these peoples do not pronounce the formula known as *tasmiya*—that is, the *Bismi Llahi al-raḥmani al-raḥim* verse ("in the name of God, He who gives mercy, the merciful")— before slaughtering the animal.[21] And even when they do so, their intention is invalidated by the suspicion of associationism that hangs over their faith.[22]

The same negative attitude predominates in what concerns marriage with women belonging to the People of the Book, with the Shi'a holding that it is not permitted to marry them except in the context of a specific union known as *nikaḥ al-mut'a*[23]— literally, a "pleasure marriage," or marriage of definite duration that dissolves on its own without a certificate of divorce at the end of a previously specified period. Not surprisingly, a marriage of this description is considered much less respectable than a traditional marriage. That these regulations are not purely theoretical but have often been strictly applied is shown in a study by Sorour Soroudi[24] that draws upon concrete examples of relations between Jews and Shi'i Muslims in Iran over the course of recent centuries.[25]

The Origins of Shiʿi Rigorism

While there have always been Shiʿi jurists who favor more moderate positions and who cite both al-Majlisi and Ayatollah Shirazi, the latter are nevertheless unanimous in desiring that the permissive position remain marginal: "All our learned jurists agree in regarding as impure at least [those] infidels who are neither Jews nor Christians and a majority of them moreover hold that even these two latter groups are also impure."[26] In this regard, two questions are critical. Which of the two positions regarding Jews and Christians—the permissive position or the strict one—may be said to correspond to the attitude of Shiʿism as it existed before the "occultation" of the twelfth and last Imam in 874? (It is to be recalled that Persia only became majority-Shiʿa with the advent of the Safavid dynasty in the sixteenth century.) Moreover, is this a question of doctrinal developments internal to Shiʿism, or must the answer be sought instead in external influences or some combination of the two?

On the first point, the Shiʿi attitude is that one should advocate separation from "the other" and consider him impure. One of the greatest Twelver Shiʿi doctors of all time, Abu Jaʿfar al-Tusi (d. 1067), explains that permissive opinions are purely circumstantial. On the one hand, they are justified by the hostility of the Sunni majority toward divergent Shiʿi legal opinions, a danger that justifies the practice of *taqiyya* (precaution), or the dissimulation of doctrinal disagreements. On the other, they represent possible recourse in cases of absolute necessity, when the believer's life is in danger. In such exceptional circumstances, it becomes lawful to consume animals ritually slaughtered by Jews and Christians or marry women from one of these groups.[27]

As for the origin—internal or external—of the notion that Jews and Christians are impure, the present state of research does not permit definite conclusions. A few hypotheses may nevertheless be advanced. Let us begin with those proposed by well-known scholars in the field of Islamic studies. In his article, "Islamisme et Parsisme," Ignác Goldziher underscored the remarkable similarities between the laws governing purity and impurity among Zoroastrians and Shi'i Muslims.[28] It is to be recalled that Zoroastrianism, the state religion under the Sassanids, was not only practiced in Persia but also throughout Mesopotamia, which was part of the Sassanian Empire. Soroudi's study mentioned above brought new data to bear on Goldziher's discoveries, showing that many of the restrictions established by Zoroastrian law to safeguard the purity of believers in contact with non-Zoroastrians or apostate Zoroastrians resemble Shi'i rules of purity to a quite remarkable degree. For example, the Zoroastrian religion forbids its faithful from sitting at table with a heretic (*druvand*) or Muslim. Consuming the meat of an animal ritually slaughtered by a Muslim is forbidden, as is consuming fat prepared by a heretic, using water or utensils touched by a heretic or Muslim, and enter into a non-Zoroastrian place of worship or touching the religious objects found there.[29]

Arent Jan Wensinck, for his part, suggested that all branches of Islam had from the outset been massively influenced by Jewish sources. This influence, he argued, may explain the rigorist positions of Shi'ism regarding the impurity of non-Muslims and the issues surrounding their food.[30] In fact, rules of ritual purity did play a major role in biblical and postbiblical Judaism prior to the destruction of the Temple, which rendered most of them obsolete, and ancient rabbinic literature added a considerable body of supplemental restrictions decreeing the impurity of non-Jews or seeking to limit interaction with them. This opinion is shared by Michael Cook, who detects Jewish influence in the Muslim legal schools that emerged in Iraq—the cradle of what is known as the "Babylonian" Talmud—and in Twelver Shiʿism, in particular.[31] Moreover, recent research by Yaakov Elman[32] and Shai Secunda[33] has demonstrated the decisive influence exerted by Zoroastrian belief, rituals, and law on the Babylonian Talmud. Within the religions practiced in the Iraqi era of nascent Islam, it is thus very difficult to disentangle where the norms specific to each end and reciprocal influence begins.

Without denying the plausibility of these two hypotheses (of the two, the first seems most likely, that of Zoroastrian influence), one may advance a third according to which the development of the doctrine of impurity was driven by concepts internal to Shiʿism. For there is reason to believe that the Shiʿi attitude toward "the other" and the need for separation emerged in response to a growing awareness of Shiʿi Muslim particularity and election. Perhaps the minority status of Shiʿism within Islam led it to develop a doctrine of election and superiority relative to Sunni Muslims and non-Muslims in a way that paralleled—but was not influenced by—rabbinic Judaism in the Diaspora. Shiʿi Muslims see themselves as belonging to a community of the elect who were chosen by God even before the sensible world had been created. This notion is expressed in several ways. According to Shiʿi doctrine, the Imams and their followers were created from a particular clay (*tina*) extracted from the Divine Throne. This "raw material" was not mixed with that from which the rest of humanity was created.[34] Furthermore, divine light traverses the Imams, who are considered to have been chosen by God. In contrast, the infidels—that is, the adversaries of Shiʿism, including other Muslims—were created from inferior and impure matter drawn from hell.[35] This self-perception as a community of the elect may explain the existence of legal rules seeking to consolidate the barriers between the elect and the rest of humanity, the pure vs. the impure. To one degree or another, Zoroastrianism and Judaism both share an attitude of this nature.

This feeling of election, and the fact of having been a perse-cuted minority throughout its history, may explain the need for isolation and separation. Mary Boyce, an eminent specialist on ancient Iranian religions, posited that a similar dynamic persists in the Zoroastrian religion, where the relationship between a the-ology of election and its various cultural and legal consequences is governed by a rigorous system of laws of purity and impurity. "The laws of purity [in Zoroastrianism]," writes Boyce, "draw their power from a doctrinal foundation based on the dualism of Zoroaster, who conceived of the world as a field of eternal con-flict between Good, to which purity obviously belongs, and Evil, which constantly jeopardizes Good and purity."[36]

In the writings of the Jewish sects of the Dead Sea, one may detect a similar dialectic between, on the one hand, a theology of election and communal superiority and, on the other, a rigor-ous system of purity laws.[37] Moreover, the possibility that Ira-nian religions influenced these writings at the dawn of the Christian era is an important theme that obviously exceeds the scope of the present discussion. Research into the comparative history of religions may shed light on other beliefs that show a dialectic of this kind. The present argument—that Shi'i rules of purity are the result of a tension intrinsic to that religion—thus does not exclude the hypothesis of external influence; it may in fact complement it.

Children of Israel: Prototypes and Evidence for the Pre-Existence of the Shi'a

In light of the foregoing, the fact that Shi'ism lays claim to exclu-sive filiation with the people of Israel does not appear so surpris-ing. This conception, that Israel is a Shi'i prototype, is expressed in the exegetical traditions attributed to the Imams Muhammad al-Baqir and Jaʿfar al-Ṣadiq. In their commentaries on the verse, "Children of Israel, remember my blessings which I bestowed on you and how I favored you over [all] created beings" (Q. 2:47), the first Imami Shiʿi commentators attributed to Imam al-Ṣadiq the idea that, at the level of the verse's esoteric meaning, the true elected people are none other than the family of the Prophet Muhammad (*ahl al-bayt*)—that is, the Shiʿi Imams.[38] The same literature contains another illustration of this identification of Muhammad's family (that is, the Imams) with the people of Israel. It is claimed that the prophet said: "I am ʿAbd Allah and my name is Aḥmad[39] and I am also the son of ʿAbd Allah and my name is Israel.[40] Everything that God has commanded of Israel, He has also commanded of me and everywhere where He refers to it, He refers to me also."[41] This tradition is based on a play of words involving the two meanings of the name ʿAbd Allah, which literally means "servant of God" but alludes to the name of the Prophet's father. Muhammad is thereby identified with Israel/Jacob, which implies that the Prophet and his descendants are a continuation of the biblical Israelites. An interpretation of this tradition is offered by al-Majlisi:

The Divine word: "Children of Israel, remember my blessings which I bestowed on you and how I favored you over [all] created beings" may be understood in the esoteric sense as referring to the family of Muhammad for [the name] Israel means *ʿabd Allah* (servant of God).[42] [According to the Ḥadith of the Prophet:] "I am the son of ʿAbd Allah and I am [also] ʿAbd Allah," as God says: "Glory be to Him who journeyed by night with His servant[43] from the Sacred Mosque to the Holy Mosque ..." (Q. 17:1). As a consequence, all positive mentions of the Children of Israel concern them at the exoteric level (*zahir*) whereas, at the esoteric level (*batin*), they concern me, and my household."[44]

Alongside this initial tendency to identify the Shiʿa with the biblical children of Israel, Twelver Shiʿi sources give expression to another attitude according to which the descendants of Israel are presented as prototypes or forerunners of the Shiʿa. Victims of Pharaoh's oppression in Egypt, the Hebrews of both the Bible and the Qurʾan are seen as the model for the Shiʿa, and their sufferings symbolize those to which the Shiʿa were subjected by their enemies. In the same way, the Hebrews' liberation from the Egyptians' yoke and their final victory over the latter are presented as a message of hope presaging the victory of Shiʿi Muslims over their enemies. The Qurʾanic foundations upon which this conception relies include the following verses:

"We shall relate to you some of the story of Moses and Pharaoh in truth, for a people who believe. Pharaoh became exalted in the land and divided its people into factions (*shiyaʿan*), seeking to weaken a party among them by slaying their sons and sparing their women. He was one of those who work corruption. We wished to show favor to those who were oppressed in the earth (*alladhina studʿifu fi-l-ard*), and to make them leaders (*aʾimma*) and to make them the inheritors (*warithuna*) and to give them a place in the land and to show Pharaoh and Haman and their hosts what they feared from them (*minhum*)." (Q. 28:3–6)

Some of the terms used here have a technical meaning for the Shiʿa, who did not hesitate to make the most of them in support of their cause. The word *aʾimma* ("leaders" or "Imams") is understood as referring to the institution of the Imamate and the various doctrines associated with it; the word *warithuna* ("inheritors") is also understood as referring to the Imams, those whom the Shiʿa considers to be the only legitimate successors to the Prophet Muhammad. In the same way, the expression *alladhina studʿifu fi-l-ard* ("to those who were oppressed in the earth") is traditionally seen as alluding to the Shiʿa, a persecuted minority throughout nearly their entire history. One of the prominent Imami Shiʿi commentators, ʿAli b. Ibrahim al-Qummi (who died over the course of the first half of the tenth century), offered the following interpretation:

God informed His Prophet [Muhammad] of the injustices and persecutions that the companions of Moses suffered at the hands of Pharaoh so that this [story] would be consolation for what he and his family were going to suffer at the hands of his own people. After this consolation, [God] told him that His Grace were bestowed upon them [i.e., he and his family] by making them His caliphs on earth and the Imams of His people. [At the end of time], He will have them return to life together with their enemies so that the latter may suffer their punishment [. . .]. God mentioned Moses and the Children of Israel as well as their enemies—Pharaoh, Haman and their troops—so that they would serve as an example [to the Shiʿa]. God said: Pharaoh killed the sons of Israel and did them harm but then God gave Moses victory over Pharaoh and his companions by annihilating the latter. In the same way, the family of God's Messenger will suffer injustice and iniquity but God will subsequently have them return to this world, them and their enemies, so that the former may kill the latter.[45]

Such parallels between the destiny of the biblical Israelites suffering under the yoke of Pharaoh and those of the Shiʿa dominated by their enemies constitute a recurrent theme in Shiʿi writings. In his Qurʾanic commentary, Abu ʿAli al-Fadl b. al-Ḥasan al-Tabrisi (d. 1153) expresses this concept in more general terms: "'We wanted to favor those who had been humiliated on earth' [...]: The just who are among us, we the household [of the Prophet] and our followers, occupy the rank of Moses and his followers while our enemies and their supporters occupy the rank of Pharaoh and his supporters."[46]

Another analogy between the fate of the people of Israel in Egypt and that of the Shi'a is established in a tradition reported by al-'Ayyashi is his commentary on the Qur'anic verse: "She [Sarah] said: 'Alas for me. Shall I bear a child when I am an old woman and this man, my husband, is an old man?'" (Q. 11:72). Muslim tradition sees these words said by Sarah, traditionally interpreted as calling into question divine omnipotence, as the reason her descendants (that is, the Israelites) were condemned to four hundred years' slavery under the Egyptian yoke. But after the Israelites repented, the tradition tells, God subtracted seventy years from their period of enslavement. According to another tradition going back to Imam al-Ṣadiq, the moral of this story is that, should the Shi'a follow the example of their Israelite predecessors by repenting, God would be lenient toward them and hasten their liberation; should they fail to do so, their suffering would carry on until it reached its prescribed end.[47]

For these authors, the biblical episode in which Gideon subjects his warriors to the test of water at Harrod's spring (Judges 7:4–8), an episode reflected in the Qur'an (Q. 2:247–250), offered another morality tale.[48] The conclusion of this Qur'anic story—"How many a small band has overcome a numerous band by God's permission. God is with the steadfast!" (Q. 2:249)—clearly contributed to perceptions of this account as constituting an additional illustration of the victory of a weak and just minority over a powerful and iniquitous majority.[49]

It is striking that Shi'i traditions of this type mainly refer to the era of Egyptian bondage and the subsequent wanderings of the children of Israel in the desert. In fact, most biblical figures chosen as paradigms also originate in this period. The same holds for the Israelites' enemies, whom the Shi'a identify with their own adversaries. Among these traditions is the famous "tradition of rank" (*hadith al-manzila*), according to which, in naming 'Ali as his successor, Muhammad said: "Your rank relative to mine is similar to that of Aaron relative to Moses."[50] In Muslim tradition, the pejorative names with which the Shi'a refer to the first three caliphs, whom they see as having usurped the place of 'Ali, draw a similar analogy: Abu Bakr is *'ijl hadhihi l-umma*, "the [golden] calf of this community"; 'Umar is *Fir'awn hadhihi l-umma*, "the Pharaoh of this community"; and 'Uthman is *Samiri hadhihi l-umma*, "the Samaritan of this community."[51] Finally, as Etan Kohlberg has shown, the title *rafida* or *rawafid*—literally, "those who reject," one of the most common appellations used to refer to the Shi'a, both by themselves and by their adversaries[52]—is among other things interpreted as reprising the title given to the seventy sons of Israel who, after having given their support to Pharaoh, rejected him (*rafadu*) when they discovered that he had renounced the true religion. They thus contributed to belief in the religion of Moses. Since then, God had reserved this title, which originally referred to a group of elect Israelites, for the Shi'a.[53]

It is my opinion that, if the Shi'a chose this period of biblical history as paradigmatic, it is because it contains two elements capable of inspiring feelings of identification: first, there is the story of a minority subjected to persecution; second, the story ends with this minority's liberation by God. In the midst of their persecution under the yoke of their enemies—that is, under the caliphs of the Umayyad and Abbasid dynasties—the Shi'a thereby gave themselves grounds for optimism.

Admittedly, the link between Shiʿism and biblical Israel as it is reflected in the traditions studied here only partly explains the Shiʿi attitude towards the Jews and their religion. Just as in Sunni Islam, Shiʿism clearly distinguishes between the biblical Children of Israel and post-biblical Jews. This distinction, which, as we have seen, has its origin in the Qurʾan itself, is already clearly marked in the terminology: whereas the former are called *banu israʾil* (Children of Israel), a term of generally positive connotation, the latter are referred to as *al-yahud*, "the Jews," a term often used in a pejorative sense. Generally speaking, the attitude towards the Jews among Muslims in general and Shiʿa in particular is heterogenous and complex. In Shiʿism, the prevailing attitude sees them as ritually impure from a legal point of view. One consequence of this attitude is that Shiʿi believers must hold themselves physically apart from Jews and abstain from consuming foods cooked by them, using utensils touched by them, contracting marriages with Jewish women, and so on. In keeping with the dualistic vision of the world that Mohammad Ali Amir-Moezzi ascribes to Shiʿism, it may also be argued that the Shiʿi attitude towards the Jews and Judaism similarly reflects this division of reality into two levels, the exoteric (*zahir*) and the esoteric (*batin*).[54] From this perspective, the laws and negative legal rules applied to the Jews constitute its exoteric facet, while the esoteric perspective allows a more positive doctrinal bent.

Conclusion

IN THIS BOOK, I have sought to survey the place occupied by the Jews and Judaism in the Qur'an while neglecting neither the historical context of the Jewish presence on the Arabian Peninsula at the time of Islam's birth nor the manner in which these Qur'anic themes lived on in later Islamic literature.

The Qur'an brings a complex dual perspective to bear on the Jews, the Hebrew Bible, and post-biblical Jewish literature. On the one hand, it is unwavering in its commitment to the Torah, the prophets and their statements, understood as divine revelations: these sources must be revered and, moreover, they attest to the authenticity of Qur'anic revelation. On the other hand, the Qur'an casts doubt on the authenticity of the Jewish Scriptures of its time and accuses the Jews of having falsified them, with the particular motive of suppressing or modifying passages that allegedly heralded the coming of Muhammad and Islam, as well as their triumph and superiority over all earlier religions, Judaism included.

The Qur'an's ambivalence toward Judaism is also marked in the domain of religious law, or *shari'a*. On the one hand, it takes abundant inspiration from Jewish *halakha*, both in term of its general concepts and in matters of detail. As is attested by many ḥadiths, on the other hand, Islamic tradition has throughout its history exhibited a desire to sharply distinguish itself from Jewish practices: "Do not resemble the Jews and Christians," "show your differences with the Jews," and so on. The goal here was to underscore the independent nature of Islam as a religion, thus obviating any need to reference the religions that preceded it.

Nowhere is this equivocal attitude more apparent than in what concerns the set of oral traditions known as the *isra'iliyyat*, a perennial source of controversy within Islam whose very name indicates their origins in the Jewish religious heritage. Many Muslim commentators have appealed to these sources and accorded them credit, in keeping with the famous ḥadith: "Narrate (traditions) concerning the Children of Israel and there is nothing objectionable (in that)" (*ḥaddithu 'an banî isra'îla wa-la ḥaraja*).[1] Others have seen in them foreign influences that absolutely required purging from Muslim tradition. They hold that these traditions were from the outset introduced into Islam by famous Jewish converts, among them the Yemenis Ka'b al-Aḥbar and Wahb ibn Munnabih, and that it would be better not to trust them.

To the degree that the Qur'an is a living, dynamic text on the basis of which Muslims regulate their lives, it is hardly astonishing that what it says about the Jews and Judaism should influence the way in which Muslims have in all times and places seen the latter. Throughout the Qur'an, which they regard as divine speech, and its fourteen-hundred-year-old exegetical tradition, Muslims are confronted with the omnipresence of Jews and their Israelite ancestors. From one verse to the next, they travel alongside and show themselves very much familiar with the issue of the election of the people of Israel, the giving of the Torah, and the entry into the Holy Land. They are similarly familiar with those who recount the divine wrath that the Jews incurred as killers of prophets, idolators, and traitors to the Covenant with God who, consequently, cannot be relied upon to honor any future alliance with men. These words from the Qur'an are present on the lips of many believers: "O you who believe, do not take the Jews and the Christians as friends. They are friends of each other" (Q. 5:51).

Muhammad's conflicted relations with the Jews of Medina beginning with his *hijra* to that town in 622—relations that so richly inform both the Qur'an and such post-Qur'anic sources as the *Sira* and the Hadith—helped fuel the negative image of the Jews. They are said to have betrayed Muhammad and to have conspired to have him assassinated. They had mocked his message and attempted to derail his mission.

It must be acknowledged that these claims are neither marginal nor limited to a group of initiates. Anyone who reads the Qur'an or listens to the sermons delivered in mosques comes to face them and the interpretation given them. If this "Jewish issue" occupies so prominent a place in contemporary Muslim discourse, it is in part because the Jews, in contrast to other groups mentioned in the Qur'an, such as the Sabaeans (who are sometimes identified with the Mandaeans, a Mesopotamian gnostic religion), are a people who still exist as a part of lived experience.

Having lived throughout Muslim history as a "protected" minority subject to the domination of Islam, the Jews came onto the international geopolitical scene with the advent of Zionism in the nineteenth century and their return to the Holy Land, followed in the mid-twentieth century by the creation of the independent State of Israel on territory that had until quite recently been an integral part of the Ottoman Empire and Caliphate. From a Muslim point of view, this situation is insufferable in both political and religious terms, for the Jews are supposed to lead a life of humiliation and poverty in the shadow of Islam.

Nor, as we have seen, is any of this entirely specific to Islam; after all, until Vatican II, the Catholic Church also held it as official doctrine that God had rejected the Jews. If the latter were to continue to exist, it should be solely as an oppressed minority underscoring the difference between the Church elected by God and the reprobate Synagogue. Conversely, while Jews and Judaism do occupy a major place in the Qur'an, they do not appear solely as antagonists, and the Jewish question is far from being central to the preoccupations of classical Muslim discourse. As we have also seen, traditional exegesis tended to focus more on specifying the circumstances in which a given verse should apply, whereas the modern tendency is to absolutize its meaning and transform it into an ideological weapon. It is the vicissitudes of history that have pushed this theme to the foreground of contemporary discourse, and it would be a mistake to conclude from what one hears today that Islam is somehow "irrevocably" anti-Jewish.

In navigating the internet, one observes a constant flow of scriptural sources, courses, and sermons that seek to draw topical lessons from the statements with which the Qur'an criticizes and delegitimizes the Jews. This incendiary discourse repeatedly mobilizes the same verses, the same hadiths. Calmer voices *are* trying to make themselves heard in the Muslim world today, but it must be recognized that they have yet to meet with much interest.

NOTES

Introduction

1. In the absence of additional information, all references in the form of Q. *XX:XX* refer to the suras and verses of the Qur'an.

2. Sidersky 1933.

3. Griffith 2013; Rubin 1999.

I: The Historical Context

1. Newby 1988, p. 7.

2. Ginzberg 1946, vol. 6, p. 432.

3. The text is quoted by C. J. Gadd in his article, "The Harran Inscription of Nabonidus," *Anatolian Studies* 8 (1958), p. 80. As Gadd notes, Iadiiu is the most obscure of all the places named in the Nabonidus inscription and cannot be identified with any known location.

4. See Robin 2012.

5. See Procopius, *History of the Wars*, Books 1 and 2, London, 1914, p. 189. For this citation, Book 1, section xx.

6. See H. Z. Hirschberg 1946, pp. 53–58; Y. Y. Toby 2018, pp. 22, 26, and 200.

7. See Toby 2018, pp. 19 and 185.

8. In Hebrew, *mikva'ot* (sing.: *mikveh*). Immersion in a *mikveh* renders ritually clean a person who has become ritually unclean through contact with a dead body (Num. 19), or through unclean flux from the body (Lev. 15) or, especially, a menstruating woman, who, before resuming intimate relations with her spouse, must immerse herself in a *mikveh* a week or so after her menstrual cycle.

9. See Jule and Galor 2015, pp. 403–405.

10. See Lecker, 2014, pp. 21–26.

11. See Goitein 1955, p. 49.

12. See Goitein 1931, p. 412. It is worth noting that the phenomenon of "*Cohanim* towns" was not specific to the Arabian Peninsula. There have been many other

examples throughout Jewish history. The Bible already mentions "the *Cohanim* town Nob" (I Samuel 22, 19). In modern times, the *Cohanim* were heavily represented on Djerba Island (Tunisia) and in the town of Debdou (Morocco).

13. Lecker 2014, p. 36.

14. Lecker 2014, p. 38.

15. See Friedlander 1910, pp. p. 251, whence Newby 1988, p. 50.

16. See Hirschfeld 1910, pp. 447–448, whence Newby 1988, p. 50.

17. Goitein 1962, pp. 146–159.

18. See Rabin 1957, pp. 112–130.

19. Zellentin's book was published in Tübingen in 2013.

20. J. Witztum's doctoral dissertation was defended at Princeton University in 2011.

21. Sharon 2017, pp. 297–357.

22. Hirschberg 1946, pp. 242–262; see in particular the discussion of its authenticity, pp. 262–264.

23. See Perlman 2012, pp. 149–169.

24. Goitein 1931 p. 143.

25. To further complicate these questions, one may note that traditional Arab historiography holds that these two kingdoms were founded by Arabs from Yemen who had fled the collapse of their ancient kingdom. For more on these questions, see de Prémare, 2002, pp. 35–81.

26. Cf. Mantran 1995, p. 86.

27. See Lecker 2014, pp. 121–177.

II: The Representation of Judaism and Jews in the Qur'an

1. All of the matters briefly mentioned here will be discussed in detail below.

2. On this accusation attributed by Islam to the Jews, unknown to pre-Islamic Jewish sources, and on the figure of 'Uzayr, see below, pp. 44–49.

3. See Ben-Shammai 2013, pp. 1–15.

4. For the story of the red heifer, see Chapter 3 below.

5. See also Chabbi 2008, pp. 347–349.

6. On the theme of Jews' transformation into apes, see also below, pp. 54–55 and notes 33 and 34.

7. See, for example, Tabari 1968, *Jami 'al-bayan*, vol. 1, part 1, p. 265.

8. See Dreyfus 1981, part 55, pp. 414–437.

9. Cf., for example, Dahan 1991, pp. 126–129.

10. See Ben-Shammai 1991, pp. 147–177.

11. See Tabari 1968, *Jami' al-bayan*, vol. 3, part 4, p. 265.

12. Cf. Bar-Asher 1999, p. 102.

13. See also verses Q. 2:93 and Q. 4:154.

14. Quoted from William Davidson's translation of the Talmud. See https://www .sefaria.org/Shabbat.88a.5?lang=bi&with=TALMUD&lang2=en [accessed 8 December 2020]. It is noteworthy that the Babylonian Talmud was completed between the late fifth century and the early sixth, that is more than a century before the advent of Islam.

15. Cf. also Katsh 1954, pp. 65–66; Reynolds 2018, p. 51.

16. See also Chabbi 2008, pp. 325–365.

17. See supra, Chap. 1.

18. Literally: "speech." And cf. "every place that the sole of your foot shall tread upon, that I have given unto you, as I said unto Moses. From the wilderness and this Lebanon even unto the great river, the river Euphrates, all the land of the Hittites, and unto the Great Sea toward the going down of the sun, shall be your coast" (Joshua 1:3–4).

19. Cf. al-Tabari's commentary on verse Q. 5:21, *Jami' al-bayan*, vol. 4, part 6, pp. 171–173.

20. Cf. for example R. Blachère on his translation of verse 58: "This verse alludes either to intrigues on the part of the Qaynuqa' Jews after the battle of Badr, or to betrayal by the Qurayza Jews during the battle of Uḥud" (Blachère 1980, p. 209, note to verse 58).

21. Ibid., p. 342, note 87. See also D. Masson's important note to his translation of the Qur'an: "The prophet Osee (VIII, 5–6) alludes to the 'calf of Samaria.' The cult of the golden calf persisted in the kingdom of the North in the time of the Kings (cf. I Kings 12:28; 2 Kings 10:29 and 17:16)" (Masson 1967, p. 885, n. 85). See also the entry *"Veau d'Or"* in *Dictionnaire du Coran*, pp. 897–899. For a superb study on this issue, see now M. Pregill, *The Golden Calf between Bible and Qur'an: Scripture, Polemic, and Exegesis from Late Antiquity to Islam* (Oxford Studies in the Abrahamic Religions), Oxford, 2020.

22. See Comerro 2005, Ayoub 1986.

23. Cf. C. Mopsik 2004.

24. al-Tha'labî 1985, p. 346.

25. The text of Ibn Ḥazm is quoted by H. Lazarus-Yafeh 1992, "Ezra-'Uzayr: The Metamorphosis of a Polemical Motif," p. 68.

26. Ibid., pp. 68–70.

27. Cf. Ben Adret 2008.

28. Noteworthy on this subject is Neuwirth's study "Qur'anic Readings of The Psalms," (Neuwirth 2009) in which she contends that the Psalms strongly influenced the Qur'an.

29. See Kofsky 2011; also Halpern Amaru 1983.

30. See Horovitz 1926, p. 40.

31. See the entry for "Crucifixion" by Daniel de Smet in *Dictionnaire du Coran*, pp. 197–199.

32. This theme is discussed below, Chap. 4.

33. For a general discussion of these themes, see Lory 2018, pp. 31–36.

34. For a discussion of these terms of metempsychosis in the context of Islam in general, see Ben-Shammai 1991.

35. The article appeared in Almog, ed. 1988, pp. 161–170.

36. *Saḥiḥ Muslim* 41: 6985 (54: 7376). See also Oliver and Steinberg 2005, pp. 19–24 ("The Gharqad Tree").

III: Biblical Accounts and Their Transformations in the Qur'an

1. According to another interpretation, widespread in Qur'anic exegesis, the word derives from the root *s-k-n* signifying "to be tranquil," "calm.". See the entry for "*sakina*" by E. G. Geoffroy in *Dictionnaire du Coran*, pp. 784–785.

2. As Geiger previously pointed out. See Geieger 1833, pp. 101–102; Blachère 1980, p. 137; Speyer 1961, pp. 84–88; Reynolds 2018, p. 199.

3. The standard text of this Mishna, which is today found, among other places, in editions of the Talmud, gives the version "a single *Jewish* person" and this has often been used to indict the Talmud for "racism." However, it must be recalled that the text of the Talmud and thus of the Mishna contained in it has since the Middle Ages been censured and "corrected" by the Catholic Church. The oldest manuscripts of the Mishna, in any case, indeed speak of "a single person" without specifying whether or not that person is Jewish. The English text cited here is taken from F. M. Young's 1898 translation of Geiger's *Was hat Mohammed aus dem Judenthume aufgenommen* (Geiger 1833), which is titled *Judaism and Islam*; for the text, see p. 81.

4. See Sidersky 1933, p. 18; Speyer 1961, pp. 84–88. A thorough analysis of the story of Abel and Cain is offered by Witztum (2011), "The Syriac Milieu of the Quran: The Recasting of the Biblical Narratives," pp. 111–153.

5. See Lory's entry for "Abraham," in *Dictionnaire du Coran*, p. 13.

6. See Gobillot's entry for "*ḥanif*," ibid., pp. 381–384.

7. See Jeffery, 1937, p. 32.

8. See also Sidersky 1933, pp. 59–61; Speyer 1961, pp. 202–203; Reynolds 2018, pp. 368–369.

9. See al-Tabari, *Jami' al-bayan*, vol. 7, part 12, pp. 187 and 189.

10. The article was published in *New Perspectives on the Qur'ān*, G. S. Reynolds (ed.), London 2011, pp. 425–448.

11. On the development of this doctrine in Islam, see Bar-Asher 1999, pp. 159–179.

12. Babylonian Talmud, *Shabbat* 56a. See also Shinan 1995.

13. See the entry for "David" in the *Dictionnaire du Coran*, p. 202. See also Z. Maghen 2007.

14. Johns 1989, pp. 225–266, especially pp. 226–227.

15. al-Tha'labi 1985, p. 265.

16. See Geiger 1833, pp. 178–180 (=*Judaism and Islam*, English translation by F. M. Young, pp. 143–144); Katsh 1954, pp. 161–171.

17. See also Sidersky 1933, pp. 109–111.

18. Blachère 1980, p. 67, note to verse 248.

19. See Katsh 1954, pp. 71–73.

20. On the *isra'iliyyat*, see among others the following studies: Heller 1928; Kister 1972; Vajda, "*Isra'iliyyat*," *Encyclopaedia of Islam*[2], vol. 5, pp. 221–222. See also Totolli 2009.

21. For the Sunni exegesis, see for example al-Tabari, *Jami 'al-bayan*, in his commentary on sura 12; for the Shi'a exegesis, see for example 'Ali b Ibrahim al-Qummi, *Tafsir al-Qummi*, al-Tayyib al-Musawi al-Jaza'iri (ed.), Najaf, 1386–1387H, vol. 1, pp. 339–358; Muḥammad b. Mas'ud al-Ayyashi, *Tafsir al-'Ayyashi*, ed. Hashim al-Rasulial-Maḥallati, Qom 1380H, vol. 2, pp. 166–201. Cf. *Genesis Rabba*, ch. 84–85.

22. See, for example, *Tafsir al-Qummi*, vol. 1, p. 85 (in his commentary on the "Throne verse" [Q. 2:255] and cf. Ezekiel, chap. 1.

IV: Qur'anic Law and Jewish Law

1. Published in *Atti della Academia Nazionlae dei Lincei*, Rome, 1975.

2. Published in *Hommage à Georges Vajda*, ed. G. Nahon and Ch. Touati, Louvain, 1980, pp. 125–134.

3. Gideon Libson has contributed an important monograph in this domain: *Jewish and Islamic Law: A Comparative Study of Custom During the Geonic Period* (Cambridge, MA, 2003). As indicated by the book's title, however, Libson above all concentrates on the development of Islam at a time when its center was no longer located in Arabia but rather in Iraq, where Jewish communities had already resided for more than a thousand years. He nevertheless devotes several pages (pp. 1–7) to its formative period.

4. Cf. Leviticus 24:19–20 and Deuteronomy 19:21; and cf. also the code of Hammurabi, law 196.

5. For a pertinent discussion of these ḥadiths, see Kister's study, "'Do Not Assimilate Yourselves . . .' (Kister 1989)

6. Rubin 2000.

7. These traditions are frequently encountered in ḥadith. See, for example, Bukhari, *Ṣaḥiḥ, Kitab al-ṣawm* (book regarding prayer), chap. 69.

8. See Goitein (1966).

9. See Katsh 1954, p. 132.

10. See, for example, in Justin Martyr, *Dialogue with Trypho*, trans. T.B. Falls, p. 30, chap. 18 §2.

11. See Torrey 1933.

12. For an in-depth study of dietary laws in Islam, see M. Cook 1986.

13. For a detailed discussion of this verse, see chap. 5 below.

14. This verse is discussed in the previous chapter.

15. Biruni, *al-Athar al-baqiya*, C. E. Sachau (ed.), p. 62.

V: The Qur'anic Sources of *Dhimma*

1. Ibn Kathir 1998, 'Umar Ibn Kathir, *Tafsir*, Beirut, vol. 4, p. 117.

2. For a detailed presentation of other Qur'anic verses considered as justifying the *dhimma* accorded non-Muslims, see Ibn Qayyim al-Jawziyya, *Aḥkam ahl al-dhimma*, Beirut, 1961, vol. 1, pp. 238–242. I discuss this text below.

3. This meaning of the word *yad* (capacity) is close to the Hebrew expression *hissiga yado* ("if he be able," literally: "his hand finds [the means]"); see, for example, Leviticus 25:49.

4. See Cohen 1994, pp. 68–72. For a detailed discussion of the exegesis of this verse, see Kister 1964; Rubin 1993.

5. C. Cahen, "*Dhimma*", *Encylopaedia of Islam*, vol. 2, p. 228.

6. The English translation of the Pact of 'Umar quoted here is taken from the magisterial volume, *A History of Jewish-Muslim Relations: From the Origins to the Present Day*, A. Meddeb and B. Stora (eds.), Princeton, 2013, pp. 72–73; see also Marc Cohen's pertinent analysis of the document (ibid., pp. 67–71).

7. For a detailed and in-depth discussion of the "Pact of 'Umar" based, among other things, on the work of Ibn Qayyim al-Jawziyya, see Cohen 1994, pp. 54–74.

8. Lewis 1984, p. 3.

9. Abitbol 1999.

10. Bat Ye'or 1985. See also Tsadik 2007; Bar-Asher 1997; Fenton 2012.

VI: The Place of Judaism and the Jews in Twelver Shi'ism

1. A large portion of what Shi'ism says regarding Jews and their religion also holds for Christians and Zoroastrians (or *majus* in Arabic). It should be noted that, despite the almost unvarying equivalence of the legal positions concerning the faithful of

these three religions, there are nevertheless differences in what concerns the Shi'i attitude towards each community. This chapter shall only consider its attitude toward Jews and their religion.

2. See, for example, Goldziher 1970; Ivanow 1948, pp. 29–30.

3. On the notion of *Verus Israel*, see above, chap. 2 and n. 39.

4. Tabari, *Jami' al-bayan*, vol. 10, pp. 105–109. It is to be noted, however, that among the traditions cited by Tabari, some distinguish between Jews and Christians, on the one hand, and other infidels or polytheists (named *mushrikun*), on the other. The former benefit from less pronounced discrimination relative to other infidels (see, for example, *ibid.*, p. 108).

5. Zaydi Shi'ism holds a position similar to that of the Twelvers concerning *ahl al-kitab*. Ismailism, meanwhile, hews to what is the most prominent current of Sunni opinion. In what concerns the Zaydis, see Toby 2018, p. 80.

6. Al-Majilisi 1983, *Bihar al-anwar*, vol. 77 p. 42ff.

7. Shirazi 1987–1989, *Mawsu'a fiqhiyya istidlaliyya*, vol. 4, p. 182ff.

8. See al-Majilisi, 1983, *Bihâr al-anwar*, vol. 77, p. 44.

9. *Ibid.*

10. *Ibid.*

11. For more details, see the references cited in the footnotes above.

12. See Shirazi 1987–1989, *Mawsu'a fiqhiyya istidlaliyya*, vol. 4, p. 184.

13. *Bihar al-anwar*, vol. 77, p. 46; Shirazi, *Mawsu'a fiqhiyya istidlaliyya*, ibid.

14. See Shirazi, *Mawsu'a fiqhiyya istidlaliyya*, pp. 194–196.

15. *Ibid.*, p. 194.

16. *Ibid.*, pp. 194–195.

17. *Ibid.*, p. 194.

18. *Bihar al-anwar*, vol. 74, p. 47. The author here cites an ancient source, the *Kitab al-mahasin* of Aḥmad b. Muḥammad al-Barqi (d. in 274/887 or 280/893).

19. This subject has been closely studied by N. Tsafrir, "The Attitude of Sunni Islam toward Jews and Christians as Reflected in Some Legal Issues" (Tsafrir 2005).

20. See Abu Ja'far al-Tusi, *Al-Tibyan fi tafsir al-qur'an*, Najaf, 1957–1981, vol. 3, p. 444.

21. Among other Qur'anic verses, see 2:173; 6:118 and 121.

22. See, for example, *Bihar al-anwar*, vol. 77, p. 43; Shirazi, *Mawsu'a fiqhiyya istidlaliyya*, vol. 4, p. 189.

23. Literally: "[Marriage of] pleasure." This is a temporary marriage, the duration of which is fixed in advance. It is only lawful in Twelver Shi'i law. On *mut'a* marriage in Shi'ism, see Gribetz 1994.

24. Soroudi 1993.

25. These questions were more recently addressed by D. Tsadik (2007), pp. 20–21 and pp. 240–241 (notes).

26. *Biḥar al-anwar*, vol. 67, p. 44; Shirazi, *Mawsu'a fiqhiyya istidlaliyya*, vol. 4, pp. 182–208.

27. See al-Tusi's formulation: "The urgency of the situation allows [the consumption of] the flesh of the [non-ritually slaughtered] animal. It even allows [the consumption of animals slaughtered] by a person hostile to Islam." (Abu Ja'far al-Tusi, *al-Istibṣar fi ma khtulifa min al-akhbar*, vol. 4, p. 88).

28. See Goldziher 1970.

29. Soroudi 1993, pp. 8–13.

30. See Wensinck, "Nadjis," *Encyclopaedia of Islam²*, vol. 7, pp. 871–872.

31. See Cook 1986.

32. Elman 2014; Skjaero and Elman 2014.

33. Secunda, ed., 2013.

34. This is the principal Shi'i stance, but it is qualified by other traditions—a tradition regarding the mixture of clays, for example (*ikhtilat al-tinatayn*). See Amir-Moezzi, p. 290.

35. On these foundations of Shi'i faith and doctrine, see for example Amir-Moezzi 1994, pp. 29–59; Bar-Asher 1999, pp. 130–140.

36. Boyce 1975, *A History of Zoroastrianism*, vol. 1 (The Early Period), pp. 295–296.

37. For laws of purity among the sects of the Dead Sea, see, for example, Schiffman 1983, pp. 161–162, 167–168, 172–173. I am here only alluding to the similarities between the messianic sects of the Dead Sea and those of Shi'ism. The subject merits study in its own right.

38. See Muḥammad b. Mas'ud al-'Ayyashi, *Tafsir al-'Ayyashi*, ed. Hashim al-Rasuli al-Maḥallati, Qom, 1380H, vol. 1, p. 44, traditions 43 and 44.

39. In Qur'an 61:5, Aḥmad is said to be a name alluding to Muḥammad.

40. The tradition refers to the biblical figure of Jacob, who was subsequently known as Israel: "Your name shall no longer be Jacob but Israel for you have striven with beings divine and human, and have prevailed" (Genesis 32:29).

41. Al-'Ayyashi, *Tafsir al-'Ayyashi*, vol. 1, p. 44.

42. This is only partly true. The Hebrew name "Israel" contains the theophoric element *el*, signifying God (Allah). But it is difficult to understand how the element *'abd* (servant) is associated with the word.

43. According to the exegetes, this occurrence of "servant" refers to Muḥammad.

44. Al-Majlisi, *Biḥar al-anwar*, vol. 24, pp. 397–398.

45. 'Ali b. Ibrahim al-Qummi, *Tafsir al-Qummi*, ed. Al-Tayyib al-Musawi al-Jaza'iri, Najaf, 1386–1387H, vol. 2, p. 134.

46. Abu 'Ali al-Fadl b. al-Ḥasan al-Tabrisi, *Majma' al-bayan fi tafsir al-Qur'an*, Beirut, n.d., vol. 5, part. 20, p. 264.

47. *Tafsir al-'Ayyashi*, vol. 2, p. 154, tradition 49.

48. It must be noted, however, that Gideon is replaced by Saul (named Talut) in the Qur'anic account; see Speyer 1961, p. 368.

49. Muḥammad b. Ya'qub Al-Kulayni, *al-Kafi*, 'A.A. Ghaffari (ed.), Tehran 1955–1957, vol. 8, pp. 292–293, tradition 498. A similar biblical account tells of how the tribe of Ephraim was posted on the fords of Jordan to put the Galaadites to the test (Judges 12:5–6). For a relevant study of this account and its possible parallels in the Qur'an, see Rubin 1999, pp. 83–99.

50. On this famous Shi'i ḥadith, see for example Friedmann 1989, pp. 58–59; M.M. Bar-Asher 1999, pp. 156–157.

51. On these pejorative appellations in Twelver exegesis, see Bar-Asher 1999, pp. 113–120.

52. In his article, "The Term Rafida in Early Imami Shi'i Usage," (Kohlberg 1979).

53. Ibid., p. 3.

54. Amir-Moezzi and C. Jambet 2018, pp. 13–18; see also Amir-Moezzi 2011, pp. 169–190, especially p. 188, n. 64.

Conclusion

1. *Saḥiḥ al-Bukhari* 3461 (book 60, ḥadith 128) and see also M. J. Kister's relevant study (Kister 1972), cited above, "*Ḥaddithu 'an bani isra'ila wa-la ḥaraja*: A Study of Early Tradition", pp. 215–239.

BIBLIOGRAPHY

Abitbol, M. *Le passé d'une discorde: juifs et Arabes du VIIe siècle à nos jours*, Paris.

Almog, S., ed. 1988. *Antisemitism through the Ages*, Oxford.

Amir-Moezzi, M. A. 1994. *The Divine Guide in Early Shi'ism: The Sources of Esotericism*, New York (=*Le guide divin dans le shi'isme originel: Au sources de l'ésotéricisme en Islam*, Paris, Lagrasse 1992, new ed. 2007).

———. 1996. "L'Imam dans le ciel: Ascension et initiation (Aspects de l'imamologie duodécimaine III)," in Amir-Moezzi, ed., *Le voyage initiatique en terre d'islam: Ascensions célestes et itinéraires spirituels*, Louvain, Paris (=*La religion discrète*, pp. 135–150).

———. 2011. "Notes on Imami *Walaya*," in Amir-Mzzi, *The Spirituality of Shi'i Islam*, London, pp. 231–275.

———. 2011. *The Spirituality of Shi'i Islam*, London (=*La religion discrète: Croyances et pratiques spirituelles dans l'islam shi'ite*, Paris, 2006).

———. ed. 2007. *Dictionnaire du Coran*, Paris.

Amir-Moezzi and C. Jambet. 2018. *What Is Shi'ism?* Abingdon (=*Qu'est-ce que le shi'isme*, Paris 2004).

Arberry, A. 1955. *The Koran Interpreted*, London.

Ayoub, M. 1986. "'Uzayr in the Qur'an and Muslin Tradition," W. M. Brinner and S. D. Ricks, eds., *Studies in Islamic and Judaic Traditions*, vol. 1, pp. 3–18.

Al-'Ayyashi, Muhammad b. Mas'ud. *Tafsir al-'Ayyashi*, Hashim al-Rasuli al-Maḥallati, ed., Qom 1380H.

Bakhos, C. and Rahim Shayegan, eds. 2010. *The Talmud in Its Iranian Context*, Tübingen.

Bar-Asher, M. M. 1999. *Scripture and Exegesis in Early Imami Shiism*, Leiden, Jerusalem.

———. 1997. "Le statut des juifs chez les malikites du Maroc," in *Relations judéo-musulmanes au Maroc: Perceptions et réalités*, M. Abitbol, ed., Paris, pp. 57–71.

Bat Ye'or. 1985. *The Dhimmi: Jews and Christians and Islam* (rev. ed., translated from the French by D. Maisel, P. Fenton, and D. Littman), London, Toronto.

Ben Adret, Shelomo. 2008. *Ma'amar 'al Ishma'el* (Dissertation on Islam), ed., Orot, Spring Valley, NY, Jerusalem.

Ben-Shammai, H. 2013. "*Suḥuf* in the Qur'an—A Loan Translation for 'Apocalypses,'" in *Exchange and Transmission across Cultural Boundaries: Philosophy, Mysticism and Science in the Mediterranean World—Proceedings of an International Workshop Held in Memory of Professor Shlomo Pines*, H. Ben-Shammai, S. Shaked, and S. Stroumsa, eds., Jerusalem, pp. 1–15.

———. 1991. "The Idea of Election in Early Islam" (=Ra'ayon ha-beḥira ba-islam ha-qadum), in *Chosen People, Elect Nation and Universal Mission* (=Ra'ayon ha-beḥira be-Israel u-va-'ammim), S. Almog and M. Heyd, eds., Jerusalem, pp. 147–177 (in Hebrew).

———. 1991. "Transmigration of the Souls in Tenth-Century Jewish Thought in the Orient" (=Gilgul neshamot ba-maḥashava ha-yehudit ba-mizraḥ ba-me'a ha-'asirit), in *Sefunot: Studies and Sources on the History of the Jewish Communities in the East*, vol. 20 (1991), pp. 118–124 (in Hebrew).

———. 1988. "Jew-Hatred in the Islamic Tradition and the Koranic Exegesis," in *Antisemitism through the Ages*, S. Almog, ed., Oxford, pp. 161–170.

Biruni, Abu Rayḥan. 1923. *al-Athar al-baqiya*, C. E. Sachau, ed., Leipzig.

Blachère, R. 1980. *Le Coran*, Paris.

Boyce, M. 1975. *A History of Zoroastrianism*, London.

Brunschvig, R. 1980. "Vœu ou serment?: Droit comparé du Judaïsme et de l'Islam," in *Hommage à Georges Vajda*, G. Nahon and C. Touati, eds., Louvain, pp. 125–134.

———. 1975. "Herméneutique normative dans le Judaïsme et dans l'Islam," in *Atti della Accademia Nazionlae dei Lincei*, Rome.

Bukhari, Muḥammad b. Isma'il. 1864. *Saḥiḥ*, Leiden.

Busse, H. 1998. *Islam, Judaism, and Christianity: Theological and Historical Affiliations*, Princeton.

Cahen, C. "Dhimma," *Encyclopaedia of Islam²*, vol. 2, 1991, pp. 227–231.

Chabbi, J. 2008. *Le Coran Décrypté: Figures bibliques en Arabie*, Paris.

Cohen, M. R. 1994. *Under Crescent and Cross: The Jews in the Middle Ages*, Princeton.

Comerro, R. 2005. "Esdras est-il le fils de Dieu?" *Arabica* 52 (2005), pp. 165–181.

Cook, M. 1986. "Early Islamic Dietary Law," *Jerusalem Studies in Arabic and Islam* 7 (1986), pp. 217–277.

Dahan, G. 1991. *La polémique chrétienne contre le judaïsme au Moyen Age*, in *Présences du judaïsme*, Paris.

Dictionnaire du Coran. 2007. Mohammed Ali Amir-Moezzi, ed., Paris.

Dozy, R. 1881. *Suppléments aux dictionnaires arabes*, Leiden.

Dreyfus, F. 1981. "Reste d'Israël," *Supplément au Dictionnaire de la Bible*, H. Cazelle and A. Feuillet, eds., Paris, pp. 414–437.

Elman, Y. 2014. "Contrasting Intellectual Trajectories: Iran and Israel in Mesopotamia," in U. Gabbay and S. Secunda, eds., *Encounters by the Rivers of Babylon: Scholarly Conversations Between Jews, Iranians and Babylonians in Antiquity*, Tübingen, pp. 7–105.

Fenton, P. 2012. *Le Pogrome de Fès ou le tritel 17–19 avril 1912*, Etude et documents, Jerusalem, 2012.

Friedlander, I. 1910. "Jews of Arabia and the Gaonate," *Jewish Quarterly Review* 1 (1910), pp. 249–257.

Friedmann, Y. 1989. *Prophecy Continuous: Aspects of Aḥmadi Religious Thoughts and Its Medieval Background*, Berkeley, London.

Furat b. Ibrahim al-Kufi. 1990. *Tafsir Furat*, Muhammad al-Kazim, ed., Tehran.

Gadd, C. J. 1958. "The Harran Inscription of Nabonidus," *Anatolian Studies* 8 (1958), pp. 35–92.

Geiger, A. 1833. *Was hat Mohammed aus dem Judenthume aufgenommen?* Bonn (=*Judaism and Islam*, F. M. Young, rans., Madras 1898).

Geoffroy E. G. 2007. "*Sakîna*," in *Dictionnaire du Coran*, pp. 784–785.

Ginzberg, L. 1946. *The Legends of the Jews*, 3rd ed., Philadelphia.

Gobillot, G. 2007. "*Ḥanîf*," in *Dictionnaire du Coran*, pp. 381–384.

Goitein, S. D. 1966. "Ramadan: The Muslim Month of Fasting," in Goitein, *Studies in Islamic History and Institutions*, Leiden, pp. 90–110.

———. 1962. "Who were Muḥammad's Main Teachers?" (=*"Mi hayu rabbotav ha-muvhaqim shel Muḥammad?"*) *Tarbiz* 23 (1962), pp. 146–159 (in Hebrew).

———. 1955. *Jews and Arabs: Their Contacts through the Ages*, New York.

———. 1931. "The Children of Israel and Their Controversy: A Study on the Qur'an" (=*"Bene Israel u-maḥloqtam: meḥqar ba-qur'an"*), *Tarbiz* 3 (1931), pp. 410–422 (in Hebrew).

———. 1931. "*Isra'iliyyat*," *Tarbiz* 6 (1931), pp. 89–101, 510–522 (in Hebrew).

Goldziher, I. 1970. "Islamisme et Parsisme," in Goldziher, *Gesammmelte Schriften*, J. De Somogyi, ed., Hildesheim (reedition), vol. 4, pp. 232–260.

Gribetz, A. 1994. *Strange Bedfellows: Mut'at al-nisa' and mut'at al-ḥajj*, Berlin.

Griffith, S. 2013. *The Bible in Arabic: The Scriptures of the "People of the Book" in the Language of Islam*, Princeton.

Halpern Amaru, B. 1983. "The Killing of the Prophets: Unravelling a Midrash," *Hebrew Union College Annual* 54 (1983), pp. 153–180.

Heller, B. 1928. "Récits et personnages bibliques dans la légende mahométane," *Revue des Etudes Juives* 85 (1928), pp. 113–136.

Hirschberg, H. Z. 1946. *The Jews in Arabia* (=*Israel ba-'Arav : Qorot Ha-Yehudim be-Ḥimyar ve-Ḥijaz*), Tel-Aviv (in Hebrew).

Hirschfeld, H. 1910. "Some Notes on Jewish Arabic Studies," *Jewish Quarterly Review* 1 (1910), pp. 447–448.

Horovitz, J. 1926. *Koranische Untersuchungen,* Berlin, Leipzig.

Ibn Kathir, Isma'il b. 'Umar 1998. *Tafsir,* Beirut.

Ibn Qayyim al-Jawziyya. 1961. *Aḥkam ahl al-dhimma,* Beirut.

Ivanow, W. 1948. *Studies in Early Persian Ismailism,* Leiden.

Jeffery, A. 1938. *The Foreign Vocabulary of the Qur'ān,* Baroda.

————. 1937. *Materials for the History of the Text of the Qur'ān,* Leiden.

Johns, A. H. 1989. "David and Batsheba: A Study in the Exegesis of a Quranic Story," *Mélanges de l'Institut dominicain d'études orientales* 19 (1989), pp. 225–266.

Jones, A. 2007. *The Qur'an,* Alan Jones, trans. 2007.

Jule, P. and K. Galor. 2015. "Zafar: Watershed of Late Pre-Islamic Culture," in *Le Judaïsme de l'Arabie Antique* (Actes du Colloque de Jérusalem, Feb. 2006), C. Robin, ed., Turnhout, pp. 387–421.

Justin Martyr. *Dialogue with Trypho,* T. B. Falls, trans., rev. with new introduction by T. P. Halton, M. Slusser, eds., Washington, 2003.

Katsh, A. I. 1954. *Judaism in Islam: Biblical and Talmudic Backgrounds of the Koran and Its Commentaries,* Philadelphia.

Kister, M. J. 1989. "Do Not Assimilate Yourselves . . . : *La Tashabbahu,*" *Jerusalem Studies in Arabic and Islam* 12 (1989), pp. 321–371.

————. 1972. "Ḥaddithu 'an bani isra'ila wa-la ḥaraja: A Study of an Early Tradition," *Israel Oriental Studies* 2 (1972), pp. 215–239.

————. 1964. "'An Yadin (Qur'an, IX/29): An Attempt at Interpretation," *Arabica* 11 (1964), pp. 272–278.

Kofsky, A. 2011. "Zechariah of Caphar-Zechariah in the Crux of Theology and Hermeneutics," *Proche-Orient Chrétien* 61 (2011), pp. 34–44.

Kohlberg, E. 1991. *Belief and Law in Imami Shi'ism,* Variorum, Aldershot.

————. 1979. "The Term Rafida in Early Imami Shi'i Usage," *Journal of the American Oriental Society* 99 (1979), pp. 1–9 (=*Belief and Law in Imami Shi'ism,* chap. IV).

Al-Kulayni, Muḥammad b. Ya'qub. 1955–1957. *al-Kafi,* A. A. Ghaffari, ed., Tehran.

Lazarus-Yafeh, H. 1992. "'Ezra - 'Uzayr: Metamorphosis of a Polemical Motif," in Lazarus-Yafeh, *Intertwined Worlds: Medieval Islam and Bible Criticism,* Princeton, pp. 50–74.

————. 1992. *Intertwined Worlds: Medieval Islam and Bible Criticism,* Princeton.

Lecker, M. 2014. *Muhammad and the Jews* (=*Muḥammad ve-ha-Yehudim*), Jerusalem (in Hebrew).

Lewis, B. 1984. *The Jews of Islam,* Princeton.

Libson, G. 2003. *Jewish and Islamic Law: A Comparative Study of Custom During the Geonic Period,* Cambridge (Mass.)

Lory, P. 2007. "Abraham," in *Dictionnaire du Coran,* pp. 9–14.

————. 2007. "David," ibid., pp. 201–203.

————. 2018. *La Dignité de l'homme face aux anges, aux animaux et aux djinns,* Paris.

Maghen, Z. 2007. "Intertwined Triangles: Remarks on the Relationship between Two Prophetic Scandals," *Jerusalem Studies in Arabic and Islam* 33 (2007), pp. 17–92.

Al-Majlisi, Muhammad Baqir. 1983. *Biḥar al-anwar*, Beirut.

Mantran, R. 1995. *L'Expansion musulmane VIIe–XIe siècle*. Paris.

Masson, D. 1967. *Le Coran: Introduction, traduction et notes*, Paris.

Mazuz, H. 2014. *The Religious and Spiritual Life of the Jews of Medina*, Leiden.

Meddeb, A., and B. Stora, eds. 2013. *A History of Jewish-Muslim Relations: From the Origins to the Present Day*, Princeton (=*Histoire des relations entre juifs et musulmans des origines à nos jours*, Paris 2013).

Mopsik, C. 1994. "La datation du *Chi'our Qomah* d'après un texte néotestamentaire," *Revue des sciences religieuses*, 68e année, n° 2 (1994), pp. 131–144; repr. in C. Mopsik, *Chemins de la cabale*, Editions de l'Eclat, Paris 2004, pp. 309–324.

Muslim, Ibn al-Ḥajjaj. 1983. *Saḥiḥ*, F. 'Abd al-Baqi, ed., Beirut.

Neuwirth, A. 2009. "Qur'anic Readings of the Psalms," in M. Anderson, *The Qur'ān in Context: Historical and Literary Investigations into the Qur'ānic Milieu*, A. Neuwirth, N. Sinai, and M. Marx, eds., Leiden, pp. 733–778.

Newby, G. D. 1988. *A History of the Jews of Arabia: From Ancient Times to Their Eclipse under Islam*, University of South Carolina Press.

Oliver, A-M. and P. F. Steinberg. 2005. *The Road to Martyr's Square: A Journey into the World of the Suicide Bomber*, Oxford.

Perlman, Y. 2012. "The Assassination of the Jewish Poetess 'Aṣma' daughter of Marwan" (=Ha-hitnaqqeshut ba-meshoreret ha-yehudiyya 'Aṣma' bint Marwan)," *Pe'amim (Studies in Oriental Jewry)* 132 (2012), pp. 149–169 (in Hebrew).

Pregill, M. 2020. *The Golden Calf between Bible and Qur'an: Scripture, Polemic, and Exegesis from Late Antiquity to Islam* (Oxford Studies in the Abrahamic Religions), Oxford.

de Prémare, A. L. 2002. *Les Fondations de l'islam: Entre écriture et histoire*, Paris, pp. 35–81.

Procopius. *History of the Wars*, Books I and II, London, 1914.

al-Qummi, 'Ali b. Ibrahim. *Tafsir al-Qummi*, al-Tayyib al-Musawi al-Jaza'iri, ed., Najaf, 1386–1387H.

Rabin, C. 1957. "Islam and the Qumran Sect," in C. Rabin, *Qumran Studies*, London, pp. 112–130.

Reynolds, G. S. 2018. *The Qur'an and the Bible: Text and Commentary*, New Haven.

———. 2010. *The Qur'an and Its Biblical Subtext*, New York and London.

Robin, C. 2012. "Arabia and Ethiopia," in *The Oxford Handbook of Late Antiquity*, S. Fitzgerald Johnson, ed., Oxford, pp. 247–332.

Rubin, U. 2015. "'Become you apes, repelled!' (Quran 7:166): The Transformaton of the Israelites into Apes and its Biblical and Midrashic Background," *Bulletin of the School of Oriental and African Studies* 78 (2015), pp. 25–40.

—————. 2000. "The Direction of Prayer in Islam: On the History of a Conflict Between Rituals" (=Kivvun ha-tefilla ba-Islam: le-toldotav shel ma'avaq bein-pulḥani), *Historia 6* (2000), pp. 5–29 (in Hebrew).

—————. 1999. *Between Bible and Qur'ān: The Children of Israel and the Islamic Self-Image*, Princeton.

—————. 1993. "Quran and *Tafsîr:* The Case of *'an yadin*," *Der Islam* 70 (1993), pp. 133–144.

Schiffman, L. H. 1983. *Sectarian Law in the Dead Sea Scrolls: Courts, Testimony and the Penal Code*, Brown Judaic Studies.

Secunda, S., ed. 2013. *The Iranian Talmud: Reading the Bavli in its Sassanian Context*, Pennsylvania.

Sharon, M. 2017. "The Decisive Battles in the Arab Conquest of Syria." *Studia Orientalia* 101 (2017), pp. 297–357.

Shinan, A. 1995. "The Image of David in Talmudic Literature" (=Demuto shel David be-sifrut ḥaza"l), in Y. Jacovitch, *David: From Shepherd to Messiaḥ* (=David—me-ro'eh le-mashiaḥ), Jerusalem, pp. 181–199 (in Hebrew).

Shirazi, Ayatu'llah Muḥammad al-Ḥusayni. 1987–1989. *Mawsu'a fiqhiyya istidlaliyya*, Beirut.

Sidersky, D. 1933. *Les origines des légendes musulmanes dans le Coran et les vies des prophètes*, Paris.

Skjaero, P.O., and Y. Elman. 2014. "Concepts of Pollution in Late Sasanian Iran: Does Pollution Need Stairs, and Does It Fill Space?" *ARAM* 26 (2014), pp. 21–45.

De Smet. 2007. *"Crucifixion,"* in *Dictionnaire du Coran*, pp. 197–199.

—————. *"Veau d'Or,"* in ibid., pp. 897–899.

Soroudi, S. 1993. "The Concept of Jewish Impurity and Its Reflection in Persian and Judeo-Persian Traditions," *Irano Judaica* 3 (1993), pp. 1–29.

Speyer, H. 1961. *Die biblischen Erzählungen im Koran*, Hildesheim 1961².

al-Tabari, Abu Ja'far Muḥammad b. Jarir. 1968. *Jami' al-bayan 'an ta'wil ay al-qur'an*, Mustafa al-Babi al-Ḥalabi, ed., Cairo.

al-Tabrisi, Abu 'Ali al-Fadl b. al-Ḥasan. n.d. *Majma' al-bayan fi tafsir al-qur'an*, Beirut.

al-Tha'labi, Abu Isḥaq Aḥmad b. Muḥammad al-Naysaburi. 1985. *Qiṣaṣ al-anbiya' al-musamma 'ara'is al-majalis*, Beirut.

Toby, Y. Y. 2018. *The Jews of Yemen under the Shade of Islam since Its Advent to Nowadays* (=Yahadut Teman be-tsel ha-Islam me-reshito ve-'ad yamenu), Jerusalem.

Totolli, R. 2009. *Biblical Prophets in the Qur'an and Muslim Literature* (Routledge Studies in the Qur'an), New York.

Torrey, C. C. 1933. *The Jewish Foundation of Islam*, New York.

Tsadik, D. 2007. *Between Foreigners and Shi'is: Nineteenth-Century Iran and its Jewish Minority*, Stanford.

Tsafrir, N. 2005. "The Attitude of Sunni Islam toward Jews and Christians as Reflected in Some Legal Issues," *al-Qantara* 26 (2005), pp. 317–336.

al-Tusi, Abu Ja'far. 1957–1981. *Al-Tibyan fi tafsir al-qur'an,* Najaf.

———. 1956–1957. *al-Istibsar fi ma khtulifa min al-akhbar,* Najaf.

Vajda, G. "Isra 'iliyyat," *Encyclopaedia of Islam*[2], vol. 4, 1990, pp. 211–212.

Wensinck, A. W. 1975. *Muhammad and the Jews of Medina,* Berlin (original in Dutch: *Mohammed en de Joden te Medina,* Leiden 1908).

———. "Nadjis," *Encyclopaedia of Islam*[2], vol. 7, 1993, p. 870.

Wieder, N. 1962. *The Judean Scrolls and Karaism,'* Leiden.

Witztum, J. 2011. "Joseph among the Ishmaelites: Q 12 in Light of Syriac Sources," in *New Perspectives on the Qur'ān,* G. S. Reynolds, ed., London, pp. 425–448.

———. 2011 "The Syriac Milieu of the Quran: The Recasting of the Biblical Narratives," PhD diss., Princeton University.

Zellentin, H. M. 2013. *The Qur'an's Legal Culture: The Didascalia Apostolorum,* Tübingen.

INDEX

A NOTE ON THE TYPE

This book has been composed in Arno, an Old-style serif typeface in the classic Venetian tradition, designed by Robert Slimbach at Adobe.